# NAVIGATING
# LIFE

# NAVIGATING

# LIFE

## FROM "WHO AM I?" TO "WHO I AM"

### K.S. WILLIAMS

MEDIA.COM

# NAVIGATING
# LIFE

The views and opinions expressed in this book are those of the author and do not necessarily reflect the official policy or position of Illumify Media Global.

Published by
Illumify Media Global
www.IllumifyMedia.com
*"Let's bring your book to life!"*

Library of Congress Control Number: 2022909282
Paperback ISBN: 978-1-955043-76-2

Typeset by Art Innovations (http://artinnovations.in/)
Cover design by Debbie Lewis

*Printed in the United States of America*

# Contents

# INTRODUCTION

"**W**HO AM I AT MY VERY ESSENCE?"

"How did I get here?"

"Where is the purpose and meaning in my life?"

If you're asking these questions, I have good news: You *can* make the journey from *existential crisis* to *existential conviction*. Within the pages of this book, I'm going to empower you to do just that.

By the way, *Navigating Life* is more than a list of steps to get you from point A to point B. It's more than a quick tool to get you out of your existential crisis. This book will guide you on a powerful journey that enables you to develop a deeper understanding of who you are and for what purpose you are here.

Be prepared to shift from a state of perplexity to a state of purpose. My hope is that you will gain a "big picture" perspective on life that will inform your essential nature. With a different perspective and fresh sense of who you are, you will gain a deeper sense of meaning, purpose, and overall life satisfaction.

## How Will We Get There?

While there is no timeline to complete your trip from *existential crisis* to *existential conviction*, you are ten chapters away. Keep in mind, though, that accessing the truths in this book isn't quite as simple as typing in your destination on your GPS and following a few arrows. The process I've developed will illuminate your path in ways you have yet to imagine. You're about to discover new and perhaps unexplored territories of your soul.

In each chapter, we will explore different aspects of your identity. We'll also navigate ways in which you may be interpreting life inaccurately, as well as identifying ways you are right on the mark in assessing what's going on. Ever wonder why the heck the world is the way it is? I'll help you make some sense out of the confusion and frustration surrounding that question too. Finally, we'll examine what makes you, *you*.

The journey from crisis to conviction will stretch and enrich your soul on multiple levels. Rest assured, you won't be making this trek alone. Not only have I had my own existential crisis, I now live with existential conviction. I finally enjoy who I am. Am I perfect? Hardly. Do I have compassion for the younger me? Without a doubt. Was the journey worth it? Absolutely.

In addition to my personal experience with an existential crisis, I have a master's in leadership that has helped me further understand three crucial questions we often grapple with: Why are we influenced to believe what we believe? Why do we operate the way we do? Who are we at our very essence?

What does this mean for you? I want to take everything I've learned and use it to help you navigate what you're going through right now. Not only will you discover a pathway out of crisis; new passageways will be illuminated to elevate and enhance your true self. You are going to become an expert in your life's story. As a result, you'll be equipped to face each day with a new level of confidence and boldly step into the future chapters waiting to be written in your book of life.

How can you get the most from this book? Befriend the feelings of uncertainty you may have as you gain your footing. Uncertainty will always exist, so embrace it and allow it to fuel curiosity instead of fear. Then, take time with the questions I present at the end of each chapter. No, the prompts are not homework; they are soul work! Then, at the end of this journey, you will find three interactive experiences that await you. They bring the teachings and insights full-circle. Plus, they are meant to be fun.

I devour a lot of books. I've read good ones, bad ones, and everything in between. I've discovered that while reading a good book is helpful, in order for it to actually become *influential* in my life, I have to make it *mine*. By that, I mean I highlight, underline, scribble, and draw on the pages. Go ahead and argue with me if it will get your mind working. When I read, I immerse myself in the experience of the words and give them a chance to develop within me.

In writing this book, I *intentionally* didn't answer some important questions for you because I am a firm believer that your life is your own. Your answers are your own. There are principles that guide us, sure, but each answer ultimately illuminates your core essence, which can only be tapped into by you. I am simply here to awaken you and get you curious. To nudge you and offer a way out of your chaotic state. That being said, I believe in honoring your story and trusting the process laid before you.

If you want to get the most out of this book and have a good return on your investment of money and time, I suggest you draw, journal about ideas with which you disagree, highlight passages, and write in the margin. In other words, interact with this content in whatever manner helps you to engage the most. I've provided blank pages at the end of each chapter where you can do all this and more.

Journaling is important because there is research that suggests people who write about upsetting events—and pull meaning from them—develop greater awareness and gain greater good from what they experienced compared to people who don't journal.[1]

My prayer has been that when you complete this book, then process and implement what you've learned, that you will be transformed and refined into a better version of yourself. I have also prayed that you will establish more certainty and security in your sense of purpose, along with confidence in your convictions. I believe you will have a deeper understanding of who you are, which will equip you to successfully interact with others and change the world with your story.

I'm honored to be on this journey with you. Let's dive in and navigate life together!

# CHAPTER 1

# WHO AM I?
# WHY AM I HERE?

*Life is not a problem to be solved,*
*but a reality to be experienced.*

—SØREN KIERKEGAARD

"So here's the deal. If you don't begin responding to your medication, you're going to have a solid chance of losing your memory in the next fifteen years."

Hearing these words from my doctor, I felt my entire life collapse. I was twenty-one and a few months away from graduating college. To say I was shocked would be an understatement. I left that appointment in complete silence, but all the while my mind was spiraling:

*Well, crap. What am I going to do? I'm supposed to graduate in three months with a very expensive piece of paper. That paper is my ticket to proving to the world I can be a part of the change!*

1

*Great. That was a waste of money and time . . . Oh, and what about all my memories of these past four years? I guess I won't remember those. Wait a minute! If I don't remember the last four years, will I even remember the next fifteen years?*

*I'll be thirty-six in fifteen years! What am I supposed to do about my dream of a family? If I pursue that, then they'll have to take care of me. My life won't be a contribution to the world; it'll be a burden. What about my friends? Should I pull away from them now and not pursue any further relationships? Is it even worth it to create memories? There seems to be no point.*

On many levels, my thoughts were ludicrous. My mind was fracturing in countless directions. I was filled with anxiety at the diagnosis of a deteriorating future.

Before this moment, I had asked, "Who am I, and why am I here?" many times (I was in college, after all). My answers had seemed obvious:

I am a friend to others.

I am a student and a tennis player.

I am a hard worker.

I am a dreamer.

I thought I knew who I was, and I had my life mapped out. I was excited about the future, even though I wasn't 100 percent sure what was to follow. My relationships were good, and my talents were developing. The future was filled with possibilities. In a nutshell: the world was my playground.

But in a heartbeat, with the devastating words of my doctor, everything changed.

None of my college courses prepared me for this moment. I was crushed. The prospect of losing all my memories changed everything. It felt like it would change *me*. Suddenly, my answers about who I was and who I was becoming were no longer satisfactory to my soul.

After many tears and conversations with my friends and family, I eventually calmed down—which was good because a body isn't meant to be in a state of prolonged shock.

But that didn't stop the questions, which rapidly flooded my mind. I needed to know who I was in light of this diagnosis. My former answers were no longer enough to help me face a future filled with an impending, devastating disability.

*Who am I, and why am I here?*

I needed to understand who I was on a deeper level, a level that was yet untapped. My inner child, equipped with Scooby-Doo detective skills, was in overdrive. So I did what many would do in my frantic situation: I got on the Internet and typed in *who am I and why am I here*. My search resulted in four billion answers.

The most common answer I found was, "Look within yourself."

Immediately, I became frustrated with the Internet's so-called wisdom. I began to ask, *Why is the Internet suggesting, "Look within yourself," when I obviously need information outside of myself because I genuinely don't know anymore? There are four billion results here. Shouldn't one of them have the answer? How am I the voice of reason amongst four billion people with working brains?*

This caused me to open up my horizons to look beyond the Internet to find the answer to life's oldest question. I needed to know the reason for my existence. My search became more urgent as I grieved the potential loss of my mind.

I then ventured into philosophy because I knew philosophers had a reputation for asking life's most challenging questions. *Surely, I will find my answers here.*

I found a debate on "*tabula rasa* versus *innatism*." Essentially, the philosophers debated whether or not the mind is a blank slate (*tabula rasa*) or the mind has certain preconceived ideas.[1] Honestly, this philosophical discourse did not enlighten me. I then went on to find a quote from nearly five hundred years ago by René Descartes that people today still deem brilliant: "I think therefore I am."[2] Apparently, being conscious is the first step to "knowing who you are," whether or not you land on the *tabula rasa* or *innatism* side of things.

After exploring philosophy, I decided to modernize my search a bit more. I looked into science. There's a permanent museum in London dedicated to the "Who am I?" question, and it involves learning about yourself through genetics, brain science, and identity.[3] Essentially, I learned that I am more than just myself; my personal experiences and relationships are a key component to informing me of who I am.

I decided flying overseas for the full museum experience wasn't in my budget, although I did purchase a genetic kit with an ancestry database. To this day, I'm still gathering information on my deceased ancestors, but I'm not sure how beneficial learning about them is to my situation. Sure, I now have some names and stories of others that are cool to share. I also have access to my DNA, which offers other health-related information. But information isn't always the equivalent of true knowledge.

I then went back in time to the wisdom of Proverbs, which says, "For as he thinks in his heart, so is he. 'Eat and drink!' he says to you, But his heart is not with you."[4] I had mixed feelings about this one. I appreciated it at first because it said I am ultimately my heart—and I had just learned I might lose my memory over the next fifteen years. So it seemed like a good place to land emotionally, at first.

However, the more I reflected on this ancient poetry, I became confused. Apparently, you are your heart, but your heart is a hypocrite. I desire to live an authentic life, you know? Also, how on earth does the heart think? I wasn't sure about that from a biological perspective.

One of my final stops (which probably should have been my first stop) was to explore psychology. I went the mental health route because asking questions without a consistent partner was less than ideal. I needed a reliable person of assistance who could handle the pace of my inquiries and provide a listening ear, as well as being able to untangle some of my thoughts.

I started working with a counselor.

In that counseling office, I discovered issues I had never even looked at, which compounded my already existing issues. These realizations were less than desirable, but I knew they were necessary. The most important thing I needed to do was grieve the idea that my identity wasn't wrapped up in my intellect or in what I could contribute to the world. Therapy was difficult, but I continued to go.

In the process, I realized I was having an existential crisis.

## What's an Existential Crisis?

Something I've learned firsthand is that when you're in the middle of an existential crisis, absolutely everything is confusing. Everything. There is no solid ground or rationale. It is a place of sifting sand.

Since *being* in an existential crisis is confusing enough, I don't want *reading* about it to add to the confusion. I am a word nerd at heart; etymology is my jam. So let me define some key words to help you understand this topic.

*Existential* derives from the Latin term *existentia*. It means "pertaining to existence; expressing or stating the fact of existence."[5] This one is fairly obvious.

The origin of the word *crisis*, however, is a bit surprising. It comes from the ancient Greek word *krisis*, which means "vitally important or decisive state of things, point at which change must come, for better or worse."[6] Only after the word was translated into English did it come to mean that something dramatic or terrible had occurred.

Having an existential crisis is neither discriminatory nor flippant. It can happen to anyone, at any time, at any age, and at any life stage. The common denominator is the questions that one often asks.

- Who am I, and why am I here?
- Do I have a purpose?
- What's the meaning of life?
- Why do things turn out the way they do?

- Why do I feel empty inside?
- How did I come to this place in life?
- What is my true identity?

These questions are obviously not for the faint of heart. They are very significant questions about the deep complexity of the human soul. The answers you find often reset and determine your foundation of existence.

An existential crisis often accompanies major events in life. Some people experience them during events society considers "good things"—like marriage, having a baby, or even having "all your dreams come true."

However, they are more often experienced during times of transition or tragedy (like mine). Common scenarios include:

- Heartbreak
- Natural disaster
- Loss of a loved one
- Job change or job loss
- Moving to a new city, state, or country
- Chronic depression or anxiety
- Loss of fundamental beliefs

If you are facing a challenging circumstance or transition, there's a good chance you're at a turning point in your life. Whether or not you're in existential-crisis mode is up for debate. But either way, you have decisions to make and changes that are about to happen.

You may find yourself mentally responding in one of two ways:

1. **This is the best thing that's ever happened to me.** Growth, transformation, and a positive perspective in life follows this thought because you believe the change is for the better.
2. **This is the worst thing that's happened to me.** Addiction, depression, and psychological breakdowns often follow this way of thinking. At best, one gets stuck in the same mindset and life patterns. At worst, their life spirals into chaos.

I believe if you're reading this today, the path of positive transformation and change is the one you are most likely traveling. Be aware, though, that the path of addiction, depression, and other tragic states is easy to go down at any point.

I've personally traveled both paths. My experience began with anxious and depressive thought spirals. But I was lucky enough to have a great support system, thanks to my friends, family, mentors, and counselor. With their help, I began to explore the path of transformation and healing.

In hindsight, my existential crisis turned out to be one of the best things that has ever happened to me. While I wouldn't classify contemplating death and disability as fun, it did open the door to asking probing questions. And anytime you find yourself asking probing questions, you're on the verge of experiencing one of life's greatest gifts:

The gift of curiosity.

## What's So Special About Being Curious?

Curiosity is one of the best, little-known magical elixirs of this world. Even Einstein believed it to be a superior way of being:

The important thing is not to stop questioning. Curiosity has its own reason for existing. One cannot help but be in awe when one contemplates the mysteries of eternity, of life, of the marvelous structure of reality. It is enough if one tries to comprehend only a little of this mystery every day.[7]

Living life with curiosity is a great way to experience this world. Being curious is something that children do naturally, mostly because they are in constant exploratory mode. They are discovering things for the first time, learning things at a rapid pace, and filling in the gaps as they go. And that is the nature of curiosity: asking questions, filling in the gaps as we go, being motivated in the quest, and being okay with getting scraped or bruised along the way.

From a scientific standpoint, when your brain becomes curious, marvelous things happen:

First, the parts of the brain that are sensitive to unpleasant conditions light up. This shows that you are slightly uncomfortable, because you recognize you are lacking certain knowledge. Then, the parts of your brain responsible for learning and memory kick into high gear, so that you can learn, and remember what you've learned, more efficiently. It is at this point that you are primed to begin your search for answers. And when you actually begin learning new facts in your curiosity state, something even more interesting than heightened memory happens: your reward circuitry kicks in.[8]

> When we are curious and allow ourselves to move past the discomfort of the unknown, it brings us to a place of *reward*.

Isn't that wild? When we are curious and allow ourselves to move past the discomfort of the unknown, it brings us to a place of *reward*. In fact, studies[9] show that we become happier and want to continue on with the reward cycle once we experience it. But even beyond scientific research and the benefits neurobiologically, this approach to life—one of a continuing dialogue of asking questions—is affirmed in Scripture too. When Christ came to earth, he taught with authority, used illustrations to draw his audience in, and lived authentically. But another key component of his life on earth was that he asked more questions than he answered. And that, I believe, was for the sake of sparking people's curiosity.

I don't believe you can ask too many questions, or that questions are only helpful during emotionally high-alert times. There is always more than meets the eye when you approach life from an inquisitive perspective.

As we age, we often feel the need to become an expert in something. I suppose that is a part of adulthood and human nature. But what if we took the posture of a kid who is exploring the world and experiencing it anew? What if asking questions could be one of life's greatest gifts to us—at any age and stage of life?

What if questions were viewed as invitations into a deeper relationship with God? What if questions were viewed as a gateway into a deeper knowledge of God, who loves us uniquely and unconditionally?

I know *What if?* can be a dangerous state of mind. But it can also be the beginning of a life filled with wonder. Being in awe is one of the greatest parts of being human. I do not envision a mundane life for you. I envision a wondrous life for you. I believe maintaining a sense of awe means embracing these kinds of questions.

Asking questions doesn't always make us feel giddy and excited, like butterflies fluttering in our stomach, nor does it provide the dopamine rush of sugar-coated candy. Even Einstein, who promoted curiosity, said, "If we knew what it was we were doing, it would not be called research, would it?"[10] That—coming from a man whose name is associated with genius—is a marvelous approach to life.

I believe the statement, "I don't know, but let's try and find out" can be a game-changer in our approach to life. Particularly when you involve yourself, God, and the community in this dopamine-seeking, never-ending search fueled by the curious mind.

Asking questions adds exponential potential into your life. To ask a question is a brave thing. It opens the door to these key personal transitions:

- Allows for a multitude of possibilities to exist, rather than a "one and done" answer
- Invites tension, whereas black-and-white concepts are easier understood but are limiting

- Gives permission for us to not have control of the answers
- Forces us to accept that our knowledge ends somewhere, allowing mystery to begin

Are those ideas scary? Are you spiraling downward into an abyss of doubt?

Please don't. Casey Tygrett, a curiosity and spiritual discipline author, writes:

> I wonder if sometimes doubt—doubt that troubles the faithful and even disconnects people from a journey of faith—is simply curiosity cast as a villain? Where else can we find language to process doubt, mystery, struggle, and even uncertainty if we have no space for curiosity?
>
> Doubt can be wonder, exploration, or the engagement of a God-wired brain in its highest gear. How can something we're wired to do become antithetical to being faithful rather than the sweetness and energy of faith itself?[11]

Just think! You could be on a pathway toward greater faith and zest for life like never before—even if you don't see it now.

## Journey into the Unknown

As Christians, we are taught to embrace a life of faith, which is trusting *what you cannot see*. Not being able to see everything ahead of us is not a bad thing. In fact, it's not even a choice—it's a fact of life for all of us.

I believe faith and curiosity are intricately linked. Both take us out of our comfort zones and stretch us like nothing else can. They chuck safety procedures out the window and ask us to step into unchartered territory.

We will begin by exploring the narratives of our lives. Constructing narratives helps us understand the world and our place in it, but these stories often go unanalyzed. Let's take a leap of faith on the journey ahead, believing that we will find the answers as we go!

## Cultivating Curiosity

1. What do you believe to be the possible cause of your current crisis? Or, if you are not in crisis mode, what do you believe has the power to shake your identity?

2. What beliefs or experiences have you currently built your life around? Write a few "I am" statements to help.

3. Do you believe that some of these doubts can lead to a good place? If so, what does that "good place" look like?

4. What do you believe will put you on the path toward growth or the path toward loss? What are your tendencies? Do you have a tendency to think of the worst-case scenarios when things are out of control? Or maybe you ignore your issues and instead keep yourself busy?

# NOTES

# NOTES

# CHAPTER 2

# WHAT NARRATIVE HAS CAPTIVATED MY HEART?

*Humans are inclined to see narratives where there are none because it can afford meaning to our lives, a form of existential problem-solving.*

—CODY C. DELISTRATY

W HAT NARRATIVE HAS CAPTIVATED MY HEART?

While this question is concise, it is actually a two-part question. It is asking both about the primitive nature of narratives in our lives and their importance within our very hearts. Before we learn some important truths about our identities—and explore why an existential crisis might be at hand—we must uncover what role we believe we are playing. Is it the one that leads to our ideal destiny? Or is it the one that sabotages our ability to find peace and uncover our true identity? The answer can be found in the narratives we've been told all our lives.

## Stories and Their Key Role in Our Lives

To put it in the most simplistic form, stories are what make us human. In every story, there's a particular way we interpret the events and give them meaning; that's the narrative. Every person has both an overarching story and narrative. They are integral to the human experience. Knowing our stories helps keep us whole rather than fractured and displaced every which way.

Storytelling has been around since the dawn of time. In fact, there are ancient cave pictures, created long before written language, that tell stories. Narratives are the vehicle that connect the past, present, and future. Our ancestors shared stories not only to remember past events, but to connect the people to the present time and give forward movement to the future. Stories allow the current generation to see the potential and possibilities that exist.

> Narratives are the vehicle that connect the past, present, and future.

Narratives and stories that have been told to us from the past influence who we are, what we think, and how we function. They tell us where we are in history. They give us a place in this big, complex world in which we live to navigate our feelings, relationships, and principles.

There are numerous ways that we consume stories. In fact, stories are all around us. People of the twenty-first century look to films, TV shows, books, audio books, plays, musicals, and even social media to follow a story. The entertainment and publishing industries bring in billions of dollars every year globally. Not only that, but with streaming services and ebook subscriptions, they can now track the weekly hours watched and read; it is not uncommon for a popular movie or TV show to reach millions of hours watched within its release week.[1]

Our money, and time, really does talk. But that still doesn't explain why we are story junkies. Seriously, we binge-watch our favorite TV show, then go to sleep, subconsciously telling ourselves even *more* stories through our dreams. Why?

Stories do a lot of things for us as a social species, and science backs this up. Let's investigate why. What happens to us when we are enthralled with a story?

## The Science and Sociology of Stories

**Stories connect people's brains**. Stories create a fancy phenomenon called *neural coupling*. This refers to how the brains of both the storyteller and the listener sync up. So let's say a coworker tells you a story about slipping on the icy road. Your brain then responds to the story as if it had happened to you. This naturally occurs between the storyteller and the listener.

Not only that, but when stories are being processed, it activates the same brain regions involved in social interactions. The stories we absorb have the capacity to act as teaching tools for us when we are eventually faced with new social situations.[2]

**Stories light up the brain like fireworks on the fourth of July—and it's a spectacular, memorable show.** They are a perfect recipe to appease various parts of the brain and its complex functions—from data-collecting to memory formation to recruiting emotional states. This means not only are we open to receiving new information, but we will also remember things better. Scientists have long said, "Neurons that fire together, wire together." When our brains are engaged in story, neurons fire up to five times more than normal. The chances of remembering increase dramatically.

**Stories change our body chemistry; therefore they change what we care about and what we act on.** When we are told an emotionally engaging story, our bodies have a variety of chemical reactions. Let's take a look at three of the primary chemicals that get activated when we are engaged in a good story:

- First, there's **cortisol**. This is the stress hormone. While stress may not be looked upon favorably, we do need a little of it for motivation. Cortisol is triggered when we perceive a threat (both real or imaginary) and provides us with necessary focus and attentiveness.[3]

- The next component is **dopamine**, which is associated with our reward system. It is most commonly known as the "feel good" hormone, as we feel pleasure when dopamine is released. When we listen to a story and stay curious and focused through the emotional plotlines, then we are rewarded with the journey of learning.

- Last, but definitely not least, is **oxytocin**. Oxytocin on its own promotes empathy and trustworthiness. This helps us to identify with the characters in the story.[4] As we continue with the story, our lives become intertwined with the destiny of the characters we relate to.

These three neurochemicals govern good storytelling and influence what we believe, motivate us to take action steps, and determine how we learn. This shows that stories are the most potent language vehicle that conveys information, knowledge, understanding, connection, belonging, meaning, and emotion into everyday life. Stories give us empathy for others, insight into our own lives, and propel us into action.

Storytelling is arguably the most powerfully persuasive vehicle of communication. It taps into our morality and decision-making processes. It can create a political realm full of peace and prosperity, yet it can just as easily produce genocide. We are moved by stories and their narratives.

Stories and narratives are the fundamental building blocks of our existence. In fact, when we embrace a story that is bigger than our own lives—a grander story of *beginning, middle,* and *end*—then we can exist as a certain character in our own lives that provides purpose and identity, even amidst the confusion and chaos of an existential crisis.

But here's the fascinating thing about stories: It doesn't matter whether the story is true or not. Fact or fantasy becomes irrelevant. We remain fully engaged when the connection with the storyteller is authentic and the message touches our own life experiences.

The world is full of stories that contain both truth and lies. The stories we relate to and the narratives we tell ourselves about the world contain bits of both, which is why it's essential to discuss what story we believe we are participating in and investing in.

## We All Have a Master Narrative

As humans, not only do we love a good story because we're literally wired for them; we also have a fundamental narrative from which we operate. This basic operative mode is called a *master narrative*. Many of us are blind to it, as these magical neurochemicals propel us into the script that we easily default to.

Master narratives are "culturally shared stories that guide thoughts, beliefs, values, and behaviors."[5] While these narratives are not indicative of one's personal story, we all live beneath them, and they deeply influence our personal stories.

Master narratives do as they suggest: act as one's "master" in life. They are a culture-centered narrative and a blueprint guide to build one's life upon. It is our internal GPS that gives meaning, purpose, and direction to each of life's stages—from infancy to death.

## What Does the Heart Have to Do with This?

From the ancient Hebrew perspective, the one thing that guides our thoughts, beliefs, values, and behaviors is the heart. The categorization that Western society prescribes to the heart, brain, and gut doesn't exist in the Old Testament biblical worldview. For the ancient Hebrews, the heart includes the emotions, attitudes, will, and motives of a person. The relationship between these would be intermingled (see the diagram on the next page).

**BELIEFS**

Our deepest convictions about life. Fundamental truth – with or without evidence. Most often associated with religion or a deeper reality.

**BEHAVIORS**

The actions and attitudes we demonstrate in life.

Our beliefs inform our behavior, and our behavior reinforces our beliefs.

Our beliefs drive what we value. When something is worth our time or attention, this drives our behavior. Our actions reinforce our behavior.

Beliefs inform values, and values inform belief.

**VALUES**

Things we assign worth to or deem "valuable" or worthy of worship.

What we value determines our behavior. Our behavior reiterates our values.

What we pay attention to most determines the value we place on it and move us to action. Our actions reinforce the cycle.

**NARRATIVES**

**The core of who we are**

Worship's fundamental to life.

Action's fundamental to life.

Our beliefs and thoughts are what make up a human being: "I think therefore I am" – René Descartes

**THOUGHTS**

The act of thinking. Thought may be an idea, an image, a sound or even an emotional feeling.

Our thoughts inform our values, and our values reiterate our thoughts.

Thoughts influence behavior and vise-versa.

Notice that each part affects the other. We think, we feel, we emote, and we move into action with our hearts. All aspects of our lives ebb and flow from this space. The heart, biblically speaking, represents the entirety of who you are.

Something that I am *not* claiming is that we *must* adopt an ancient understanding. However, there are benefits to looking at things through a different lens. For example, adopting the ancient Hebraic perspective lends itself to recent and ongoing scientific discoveries, such as:

- The brain is not limited to how we think. As I mentioned earlier, it links us with other humans, which—in turn—influences our human behavior.
- Human behavior is always linked to emotion. In fact, if we took emotion out of the mix, we would no longer be in-motion. We would stop moving.
- Emotion is the undercurrent of human thought process. While emotion is displayed more in certain areas of the brain, it is almost always a part of the equation of thinking (even if it is subconscious).[6]

All this to say, our hearts are synonymous with the narratives we believe. We biologically absorb stories and then biographically walk them out into the world.

> The stories we carry and the stories we tell all come from our heart.

The stories we carry and the stories we tell all come from our heart.

It is essential to mention that while our "below the surface" selves are integral to who we are, they are still not without their own biases. But why is that? One reason is that culture—whether our cultural beliefs are based on truth, misperceptions, or lies—

is central to the narratives of our hearts. These narratives are shared so often through every part of culture—home, media, educational and religious institutions, to name a few—that they become invisible. They are self-reinforcing; therefore we can almost robotically walk them out. The second feature is the fact that the majority of our stories are formed in the invisible reality of the heart. Our thoughts, beliefs, and values are solidified below the surface of ourselves. Understanding and uncovering the invisible realities beneath the surface is the key to finding out who we believe we are, and the story we believe we occupy.

The heart has several characteristics—other than thoughts, feelings, attitudes, and emotions—that greatly impact our understanding of ourselves and our lives. There are three key biblical texts regarding our hearts that can help illuminate the narratives we believe:

- "Above everything else guard your heart, because from it flow the springs of life." (Proverbs 4:23 isv)
- "The heart is deceitful above all things, and desperately sick; who can understand it?" (Jeremiah 17:9 esv)
- "All these evil things come from within, and they defile a person." (Mark 7:23 esv)

This means that the heart has paradoxical qualities: the very essence of life flows from it, but so does evil. While it's true that the heart cannot be ignored, our heart is sick and easily misled. This common interpretation has often led to the cultural Christian saying: "Follow your head, not your heart."

The result of this mantra often translates as, "Follow what is factual, not your feelings." And when we actually practice this mantra, it often results in ignoring our feelings. Instead, we stuff ourselves with information to produce rationalized thoughts, compensating for our false feelings.

I am afraid this common Western phrase has resulted in a fallacy that has done a disservice in understanding who we are. No human can be reduced to the neurological activity between the six inches of space in our heads that represent these "facts" or "rational thoughts."

I am afraid many of the older generation (which is where much of this message derives) have reduced their identities to their reasonability, facts, and intellect. And the result of this has been an unhealthy and emotionally suppressed existence. I worry that a large percentage of the upcoming generation who focuses primarily on elevating their emotions will result in a heedless existence, leaving many feeling empty and unfulfilled. Your emotions are not your identity-markers, so putting too much weight and attention to them will lead you astray. Reducing yourself to either logic or feelings isn't the right approach to life.

From both the ancient Hebrew perspective and ongoing scientific research, knowledge is not to be separated from feelings, nor are feelings to be separated from knowledge. We are designed as humans to be integral (meaning whole) human beings.

Integration requires us to acknowledge both the rational and the emotional aspects of the human heart. Otherwise, we are ignoring God-given signals to indicate to us what we believe. Even if our signals are wrong because they have believed lies, at least that is a starting point. What we really believe about ourselves and this world leads us into knowing who we believe we are—at the very least.

The perceived "facts" one believes could be wrong, just as your feelings could be wrong. Or they could both be right. Is it possible we have followed the wrong feelings or the wrong thoughts this whole time? Have our hearts held things as a treasure? Things that are, in fact, trash? Whether we like it or not, we are each guided by our heart, which often acts as a faulty compass that can lead us to both life and death.

So what is one to do with such a dilemma? What can we make of these stories that have given us purpose that might, in fact, be filled with falsehoods? We must continue our curiosity journey. We must uncloak the master narratives of our hearts and, in turn, discover the "truths" that we believe, even if they are lies in disguise.

## Cultivating Curiosity

1. What movies, books, or other forms of media do you digest *willingly*? Why?

2. Are there any thoughts, beliefs, values, and behaviors that you've second-guessed in life but followed anyway due to societal expectations?

3. Look at the heart diagram in this chapter, then examine what values, beliefs, behaviors, and thoughts reside in your heart.

4. What is your current relationship between your thoughts and your feelings? Do you believe it to be the best view, or should you consider other alternatives?

5. Much of Christianity has recently focused on "renewing the mind" and has been heavily influenced by neuroscience. What do you think about "renewing the mind" in light of the above?

6. Do you believe the biblical heart has a physical location, or is immaterial? Why do you believe this?

# NOTES

# NOTES

# CHAPTER 3

# WHO DOES MY CULTURE SAY THAT I AM?

*Life can only be understood backwards;*
*but it must be lived forwards.*

—SØREN KIERKEGAARD

WHEN UNCLOAKING A MASTER NARRATIVE, IT IS IMPORTANT to understand the general interpretation of the historical events that have taken place. When we comprehend the most common interpretation of events, we can eventually get down to the master narrative. In turn, we can uncover what is good, bad, and neutral about our lives.

## A Tumultuous Beginning

July 4, 1776, is the most well-known date in United States history. While today we celebrate with food, fireworks, family, friends, and fun, the day first held a very different feeling. The King of England had been relentless in his tyranny over the previous decade. The Americans had grown weary of the ever-increasing burdens that had been placed on them over the years without appropriate representation in the British Parliament, including, but not limited to:

- 1765: The Quartering Act (forced colonists to provide housing, food, and clothing for British troops)
- 1767: Townshend Acts (tax on tea, lead, paint, glass, and paper)
- 1773: Tea Act (created a monopoly for British tea, since they were the only company allowed to distribute and sell tea to the colonies)[1]

Meanwhile, on the other side of the pond in England, King George III believed he had proper and just authority in taxing the American colonies. The colonists disagreed and were vehemently angry. While the first battle of the Revolutionary War was in 1775, it wasn't until 1776 that America told King George III how much of a terrible tyrannical toddler he had become over the years. He was unjustly using his power for personal gain.

This was a bold and rebellious move because—from the king's perspective—he was just making the Americans pay for the British defending them in the French and Indian War. The Americans were seen as ungrateful, pitiful children in his eyes.

These "pitiful" children of the colonies didn't care. They'd had enough mistreatment without proper voting rights. Americans believed that, regardless of what authority might be over you, respect and the right to be heard were foundational to the human experience. Fundamental to humanity is the right of speech, the right of opinion, and the right to overthrow any power that denies these rights.

America declared its independence boldly. Not only did they list the many reasons King George III was an abomination to power over the American colonies, but the document also coined a key phrase that abides in many American hearts today: "All men are created equal, that they are endowed by their Creator with certain unalienable Rights, that among these are Life, Liberty and the pursuit of Happiness."

With these words, along with a feisty and rebellious spirit, the American colonies marched into war with England. It was a war marked with the scrappiness and valor of the young and rebellious nation. America finally won, several years after its declaration, in the autumn of 1783.

And the rest is history. The American spirit developed from a mindset of the equality of opportunity and personhood. The American spirit is one of grit, daring bravery, and advancement. No challenge is too large, no opportunity too grand. America defeated a long-reigning world power. In this new quest of life, liberty, and happiness, no stone would go unturned.

## The Progress of America: Establishing Law and Continuing West

After America had won against Great Britain, they took the lessons learned and put them into law. The founders believed it necessary to permit its citizens to have weapons for protection against the governmental authorities. Why? Because any ruling authority has potential for corruption. The opportunity to rebel (even in a new established government) needed to be granted and secured. It was also important that power between branches of government was balanced. America had seen that the government could be corrupt with power and greed, but with divided power paired with necessary accountability, perhaps America could become the greatest nation to ever exist.

Since America had just beat a power that had held them back for years and treated them atrociously, it was now time to move forward in hope. Now was the time to provide ways for Americans to pursue its newly declared rights of life, liberty, and happiness—no matter a person's class distinction. This was an opportunity like no other, because America was a new and emerging nation. Nobility and classes didn't matter. Bloodline rights were not a thing; it was one's own grit and effort that dictated one's chances of a great life. We had won the battle for freedom, but now we faced the challenge of defining the fullest life possible.

> We had won the battle for freedom, but now we faced the challenge of defining the fullest life possible.

In 1803, President Jefferson purchased Louisiana from France. This doubled the size of the United States and increased opportunities for the lives of its citizens. Land was associated with wealth back then, much like it is today. Jefferson believed that this expansion was the key to the young nation's growing population, as well as the growing demands for a better life and, ultimately, prosperity. By 1840, about seven million Americans—nearly 40 percent of the United States' population—resided in this new territory for the purpose of building a new life for themselves and their families.

In 1843, the Great Emigration to the Oregon Trail began. The association of moving for the purposes of progress, land ownership, freedom, independence, and upward mobility grew. In 1845, a journalist coined the phrase "Manifest Destiny" to describe "the idea that the United States is destined—by God, its advocates believed—to expand its dominion and spread democracy and capitalism across the entire North American continent."[2]

While this idea wasn't fully accepted by all Americans, the notion did embed itself into our country. While Europe seemed characterized at the time by factories and the working class, that was far from the American reality. The American reality was that of a dream—an utmost potential to be realized and beauty and happiness to be had.

With this idea in hand, America kept moving toward an open landscape with open possibilities and exponential potential. In early 1848, gold was found in California. While the initial founders attempted to keep it a secret, the word spread as fast as it could. People rushed from across the nation and the world to seize a kind of wealth and lifestyle they would've never imagined. It was a wild time where "survival of the fittest" was the common theme. By the end of 1849, an estimated one hundred thousand nonnative people were in California; the previous year it had been only twenty thousand. Over the next several years, two billion dollars of precious metals were unearthed in the mines.[3]

Even though Americans had struck gold, the dream of land ownership and wealth was far from fulfilled. On July 4, 1861, President Abraham Lincoln told the United States that the government was "to evaluate the condition of men, to lift artificial burdens from all shoulders and to give everyone an unfettered start and a fair chance in the race of life."

That furthered the American spirit of competitiveness and hustle, and President Lincoln soon followed with the Homestead Act in 1862, which permitted all citizens from all walks of life (including slaves, women, and immigrants) to become landowners. The law was in place until 1976, during which 270 million acres of land were given to Americans for a small filing fee.

The Pacific Railroad Act was passed in 1862 as well, and the dream of connecting the East Coast and the West Coast was closer to becoming a reality. The mandate was given to two railroad companies (the Central Pacific and the Union Pacific Railroad) to "meet in the middle."

Each company was given land and government bonds for every mile of new track that they laid. This not only provided motivation, it also created competition between the railroad companies to acquire the most money and land. Both companies faced challenges, including crossing rugged mountains and Native American settlements.[4]

The American experiment—the growing spirit of conquest, the unbridled pursuit of opportunity, and the belief in unfathomable potential to live big—came at the expense of others. In particular, it came at the expense of the Native Americans' lives and their land.[5] In the name of "Manifest Destiny," American people excused their sins. It was survival of the fittest, and those who survived perceived themselves destined to do so.

## The American Dream and Its Continued Evolution

While the concept of the American Dream can be traced back to the birth of America and the beliefs of its Founding Fathers, it wasn't until 1931 that there was an official definition. Historian James Truslow Adams in his book *Epic of America* wrote: "The American Dream is that dream of a land in which life should be better and richer and fuller for everyone, with opportunity for each according to ability or achievement."[6]

According to Adams, the American Dream is not something that is seen as simply self-indulgent in nature; instead, it's something that, when connected with a democracy, promotes social well-being. Adams goes on to say that the American Dream is not "a dream of motor cars and high wages merely, but a dream of social order in which each man and each woman shall be able to attain to the fullest stature of which they are innately capable, and be recognized by others for what they are, regardless of the fortuitous circumstances of birth or position."[7]

Adams's definition echoes the Declaration of Independence, the Homestead Act, and the Pacific Railway Act—three documents that also put forth the idea that Americans should pursue a life of potential not yet realized.

Americans worked hard because of the opportunity and the potential life that lay before them. This continued in different ways into the late twentieth century, when getting an education, owning a home, and collecting lots of "stuff" were considered the hallmarks of success.

Today, the American Dream can now be bought on credit. We incur student loans to land that coveted education. We take out mortgages for big homes we cannot afford. We apply for credit cards to buy more stuff.

For some, the American Dream might look like having a six-figure salary with no serious work obligations. For others, it means lavish clothes, expensive vacations, or the best schools for their kids. Still, others desire fame in the form of "overnight social media sensations" and viral notoriety, making others believe that they can "make it" as well.

As a nation, we accumulate stuff like no other. We seem to be the biggest hoarders, accumulating 2.3 billion square feet of stuff, which is nearly three times the size of Manhattan. While 65 percent of renters have a garage, attic, or basement for storage, there is no extra space. Many Americans live beyond their means by accumulating worldly possessions.[8]

Today's American Dream might look slightly different today than it did two hundred years ago (after all, there were no overnight Internet sensations in the 1800s), but at its roots, the idea is the same. The American Dream continues to be obsessed with progress and potential, often embodied through materialism or euphoric ecstasy.

We believe that in each generation we will realize greater liberty, freedom, and happiness. Even if there is no land to be found, there is opportunity to be seized somewhere. Technology, capitalism, and competition has sped up the process.

## What Does History Unveil About Our Beliefs?

While recent political agendas and news outlets would suggest that we are the "Divided States of America" rather than the United States of America, our history suggests we do, in fact, have a master narrative that holds society together. We do, indeed, have "culturally shared stories that guide thoughts, beliefs, values, and behaviors."

The American Dream and its evolution are still strong parts of America and the stories that we share. The stories we love consist of rags to riches, triumph over tragedy, and the underdog overcoming the giant of the day. We love a good upset of any sporting event, just like the foundation of our nation. We love stories that defy the majority—particularly because we have a heart of rebellion for any leadership that is not our own. We love stories that are magical because we believe there's always more to life than meets the eye. We love stories that have happy endings because that's the life we want. As a nation, we feel any conflict is worth it as long as a comfortable, independent, and happy life is the endgame.

And all of these shared stories do indeed suggest how one should *be* in society. However, that is not our only commonality. After traveling to nearly twenty countries, there is one thing I've noticed that Americans have in their veins that isn't simply the American Dream brought about by the oppression of a tyrannical king: the idea of *individualism.*

Individualism is a philosophical movement that has seemed to birth much of the Western world. Individualism "endorses the principle that the ends or purposes of the human individual possess dignity and worth that take precedence over communal, metaphysical, cosmological, or religious priorities."[9]

While individualism has taken on various forms in other countries, it was particularly suited to America and its rebellious history. Individualism has become intertwined in America's ethical, political, and social values of democracy, capitalism, and the separation of church and state.

From an ethical perspective, individualism has shifted into what an individual's conscience believes. While it says "In God We Trust" on our currency, the Founding Fathers did not explicitly say which God that is or what specific behavior was appropriate. It simply implied that no one should be a god themself. Everyone should be equal in liberty and power.

Individualism, since invading our ethical decision-making, has no sphere it hasn't touched. It is rampant in every sphere in society one can think of—from social systems, to educational realms, to commerce, and the political institutions. Now we excuse our sins due to inconveniences in our life, or something that does not match our own personal conscience. In an effort to elevate the individual above everything else, individualism has become America's religion of choice.

> In an effort to elevate the individual above everything else, individualism has become America's religion of choice.

On the positive side, this has created a culture in America in which competition and creativity are some of the best when paired with a capitalist society. We have strong sporting competitions, innovative minds, and the freedom of self-expression, which has created the likes of Disney and Hollywood. On the negative side, all this autonomy has gone against how we are wired to connect with others. While autonomy can be the breeding ground for innovation and competition, it can also be the breeding ground for loneliness. American society has reached epidemic levels of loneliness in recent history. Numerous studies suggest that each generation is lonelier than the preceding one.[10]

## Is There a Different Narrative?

The American master narrative, with all of its grander and idealism, falls dramatically short at the end of the day. America's narrative of political and social culture that values autonomy, progression, and self-reliance is impressive. But like all master narratives, it leaves many people out. The ramifications aren't just seen in our loneliness levels. The result is, in fact, not equality; it's inequality or, at worst, discrimination.

As the American story loves productivity, control, innovation, and change, this leaves out a huge demographic. Dying people, for example, are not productive in the slightest. They are needy consumers, not contributors to society. Being terminally ill not only represents losing one's value of autonomy, control, and independence but also the recognition of our human limitations. Our doctors were not innovative enough or smart enough to control death. In the American narrative, death is the epitome of shameful loss.

The American story also leaves out people who might not deem it necessary to go into student debt for a "better future." Those who, while they may want autonomy, have no real clue who they are or what they want to do for the rest of their lives. It also leaves out the value of newborns because—heck—they are dependent on everyone and are a personal liability to freedom and independence. The American narrative doesn't include those with disabilities because they aren't autonomous. It doesn't include someone who is simply content in life and maybe doesn't feel obligated to chase "progress."

While America's master narrative—and any other culture's master narrative—has its reason for existing, there are some major flaws. Sure, they provide societal unity that "moves us along" in life. But at the same time, these narratives also suggest that if we do not follow its blueprint, then parts of our lives are not worthy of being shared, known, or loved. These narratives propose that anyone outside of its blueprint do not live a noteworthy life.

There must be a narrative that can include everyone—from those with disabilities, the terminally ill, minorities, or those we deem "less valuable" in society. We need a story that values one's life from infancy to death, for all socioeconomic groups, races, and genders. We need a narrative in which no bit of life goes to waste.

I have found a counternarrative to America's master narratives (and those of other cultures too). It displays truth cross-culturally and encompasses all people. It is the beginning of an epic in which everyone can find their identity, purpose, and value—no matter who you are or where you come from.

## Cultivating Curiosity

1. Whatever place you call home, what do you believe the master narrative of your country is when looking back at the history and the cultural stories of acceptance? What does your localized culture (and the culture of your country) suggest your role in life should be?

2. If you were to replace the USA's presented master narrative with a different one, could you explain the narrative that would include everyone and not ostracize anyone?

3. Which piece of society do you believe contributes most to the narratives in our lives and why?

4. What do you believe is the relationship between the kingdom of God and politics?

5. Every culture is filled with half-truths (lies). Where are some half-truths in your culture?

# NOTES

# NOTES

# CHAPTER 4

# WHAT DOES A TALKING SNAKE HAVE TO DO WITH IT?

*Stories matter. Many stories matter. Stories have been used to dispossess and to malign, but stories can also be used to empower and to humanize. Stories can break the dignity of a people, but stories can also repair that broken dignity.*

—ANNIE ADICHIE

FOR OUR MASTER NARRATIVE, WE ARE GOING BACK IN TIME. Way back—to the beginning. This story contains the master narrative of all narratives. It shows a world of dignified, empowered, whole humans and their Creator, King of kings, Lord of lords—the Master of all creation.

The setting begins in a world where tarnished hearts and convoluted narratives are not yet a piece of the puzzle. The setting is described throughout the book of Genesis. The first two chapters of Genesis paint a picture of paradise on earth. We see God's original intention for the world.

In the third chapter of Genesis, we read about sickness and evil embedding itself in the story, resulting in distorted beliefs regarding ourselves, God, and the world. In the invasion of evil, we see the roots of our contaminated, confused, and chaotic lives. It isn't the end of all endings though. There is foreshadowing of a Hero who will come along out of his great love for us and restore what has been broken.

If we can grasp these first three chapters in Genesis, we have the etchings of a new master narrative. These chapters are the fundamental building blocks to our identity and the characters we represent in the grander story.

## Genesis 1

Genesis 1 is not necessarily a riveting read, but it is a rhythmic one.

The opening words of the Bible in Genesis 1:1 say, "In the beginning God created the heavens and the earth." In essence, God created everything.

In the first two days of creation, this occurred:

> And God said, 'Let there be light,' and there was light. And God saw that the light was good. And God separated the light from the darkness. God called the light 'day,' and the darkness he called 'night.' And there was evening, and there was morning—the first day. And God said, 'Let there be a vault between the waters to separate water from water.' So God made the vault and separated the water under the vault from the water above it. And it was so. God called

the vault "sky." And there was evening, and there was morning—the second day. (Genesis 1:3–8)

Throughout the first chapter of the Bible, we begin to see a powerful pattern:

## 1. God speaks things into existence.

God's words possess incredible power. His words exude creativity, unity, and exponential power and authority. They literally hold the world together.

## 2. God judges what has been made as good.

As God is creating his work, he acts as a judge and deems it *good*. Oftentimes, *good* elsewhere in the Bible is treaty language that emphasizes agreement and loyalty between the parties. Here, the word *good* places emphasis on what God creates. It is in harmony with his morality and divine goodness.

## 3. God gives what he creates a name.

In Hebrew, the name most often assigns a particular function or purpose; it gives a person or thing a distinguished identity. Have you ever not liked a name because of its connotation? There's a reason for that. From this, it is clear that the God of the Bible creates narratives of goodness, order, and authority.

On the sixth day, God does something different. God creates humanity, but it's in a very unique manner. The story told in Genesis 1:26–27 continues:

Then God said, 'Let us make mankind in our image, in our likeness, so that they may rule over the fish in the sea and the birds in the sky, over the livestock and all the wild animals, and over all the creatures that move along the ground.' So God created mankind in his own image, in the image of God he created them; male and female he created them.

Many religions through time have embraced their own creation stories. But the Bible is distinct in that it drives home this powerful point: men and women are no afterthought. God says that all humans—not just privileged people—are made in the image of God. Being made in the image of God is the great equalizer of humanity for all races, cultures, socioeconomic groups, and genders. It is the epitome of democratized humanity.

I know how blissful that sounds.

And guess what? God's story about his love for humanity gets even better when we look at the original language and audience.

God placing his own image (*tselem*) and likeness (*demut*) in humanity shows the highest possible regard for a created creature. Both words, image and likeness, are synonyms and refer to something that is similar—but not precisely—the thing that it represents.

One of the translations of *tselem* is "a shadow." A shadow does not necessarily look exactly like you, but it behaves like you and is representative of your actions. This is how the Hebrews thought: being made in the image and likeness is not representative of a person's physical appearance; instead, is representative of a thing or person's functionality—the purpose, intention, and thoughts behind it.[1]

*Tselem* can also be translated into "idol" or "statue." Idols were used to represent the power and presence of a particular god in those times; a statue was often used to display a king's authority and elicit obedience and worship. Being made in the "image of God"—or *tzelem elohim*—was a phrase that at the time was only designated for kings.[2]

The royals at that time had a very distinguished role to play, much different than modernized monarchy. Not only were the royals the visible representatives of the invisible God, but they were also the intermediary between the gods and the world. They issued decrees according to the wills of the gods and asked for blessings for their kingdoms.

> You are democratized royalty in the flesh.

By God creating you in his image, he's saying that you are the equivalent, if not better than, royalty. Men and women, your role in this world is to be the royal representatives of God on earth. That's right! You are royalty. You are democratized royalty in the flesh.

If God wasn't clear enough about humankind being made in his image, he clarifies our royal status and duties even further by saying, "Be fruitful and multiply and fill the earth and subdue it, and have dominion over the fish of the sea and over the birds of the heavens and over every living thing that moves on the earth" (Genesis 1:28 ESV).

So not only is our God the Creator of all things, he also creates good things. He's a God of deep abundance and generosity, desiring for us as his representatives to multiply the good things in this world.

"Subdue" in Hebrew is *kabash*, and its meaning differs greatly. In its worst instances, it can mean "enslave, molest, or rape." In a military context, *kabash* means "to place your foot on the neck of your conquered enemy" to signify submission of that enemy.[3] On the more positive end, *kabash* translates to "bringing something under control that is wild, bringing something into proper working order so that it flourishes."[4]

But when "subdue" is coupled with "rule or have dominion," the meaning is clearer. To have dominion or rule is the Hebrew verb *radah*. Again, this is the language meant for royalty. Benner notes, "*Radah* is related to other words which have the meanings of descend, go down, wander and spread. This verb literally means to rule by going down and walking among the subjects as an equal."[5]

In other words, God's royal representatives rule with humility. It embodies a heart-attitude of care and equality, a devotion to the expansion of goodness and beauty, and a commitment to accurately representing the invisible God.

## Genesis 2

I really love the first couple chapters of the Bible. Many Bible stories are documented in other historical books, providing different perspectives, but there is nothing that compares to Genesis chapters 1 and 2. Chapter 2 gives us details about our royal role on earth. In this narrative, God further expands how to be his faithful representative. He places the man in the garden to "work it and take care of it" (v. 15). In Hebrew terms, we are to *abad* and *shamar*.

*Abad* means "to serve" in a way that is cultivating. A central part of our royal identity is work. We're designed to reflect *good creative work*, like God. And when we work, we serve. Working and serving are intertwined, not mutually exclusive. *Abad* also entails cultivating something. It entails making things better, improving on what already exists, embellishing, or even adorning. *Shamar* means "to take great care of, guard, protect, or sustain." When we are God's royal representatives, we take care of our surroundings in a way that preserves its beauty—and even enhances it.[6]

As these verbs are coupled, this reiterates that we were created with great power but not in a dictatorial way. We are not to use the world for our own selfish ambitions. As God's royal representatives, we are called to exercise our authority to serve, protect, and enhance the world.

While Eden was already a beautiful place with four rivers, accented with gold and other precious stones, there was still room for improvement. God created the world in a way that if we do not participate in the story according to our divine responsibility, it is not complete. It's necessary that we collaborate with God and one another to bring the world into its full potential.

As the Bible shows us, God continues to refine the image-bearer's role by telling Adam: "You are free to eat from any tree in the garden; but you must not eat from the tree of the knowledge of good and evil, for when you eat from it you will certainly die" (v. 16).

It is clear: we are created with authority and under authority.

Genesis 2 continues to show Adam exercising dominion as God has asked. Adam is exercising his authority while under authority. God brings the animals to Adam, and whatever Adam names them, that is their name. It appears to be an excellent team-building experience for both Adam and God.

But creation is not quite finished. God assesses that Adam is lonely in his image-bearing duties and God declares it is *not good*. God's story is consistent in being completely good. So God—being the master artist and gift-giver—comes up with a creative plan.

God performs the world's first documented surgery, putting Adam into a divine nap and creating woman from the side of man. Adam wakes up to a naked woman and says, "This is now bone of my bones and flesh of my flesh; she shall be called 'woman,' because she was taken out of man" (v. 23).

Man's need for another was met with the woman; and woman's need for another was met with the man. Creation was now complete.

Genesis 2:24–25 finishes, "Therefore a man shall leave his father and his mother and hold fast to his wife, and they shall become one flesh. And the man and his wife were both naked and were not ashamed" (ESV).

As we see, "paradise" is complete when we are known and loved in our relationships with one another and with God, exercising our rulership with humility, and working and serving others and our world.

## Genesis 3

Genesis 3 is when our narratives get twisted, our dignity becomes broken, and our hearts become infiltrated. It begins abruptly with a new character:

> Now the serpent was more crafty than any other beast of the field that the LORD God had made. He said to the woman, "'Did God really say, 'You shall not eat from any tree in the garden'?'" (v. 1 ESV).

Up until this point, the serpent is the only creature that has questioned God's authoritative word. The story continues in verses 2–3 with the woman replying, "We may eat fruit from the trees in the garden, but God did say, 'You must not eat fruit from the tree that is in the middle of the garden, and you must not touch it, or you will die.'"

The woman misquotes God's words. There's no explanation as to whether she misheard God or simply forgot what he had said. It remains a mystery. Either way, the serpent sees the misquote as an invitation for an alternative narrative and quickly offers one:

"'You will not certainly die,' the serpent said to the woman. 'For God knows that when you eat from it your eyes will be opened, and you will be like God, knowing good and evil'" (vv. 4–5).

The serpent slinks forward strategically, from initially questioning God's authority, to spinning a completely different narrative. The serpent's offer appears to be an attractive alternative to the instruction God had given. Chapter 3 continues in verses 6–7:

When the woman saw that the fruit of the tree was good for food and pleasing to the eye, and also desirable for gaining wisdom, she took some and ate it. She also gave some to her husband, who was with her, and he ate it. Then the eyes of both of them were opened, and they realized they were naked; so they sewed fig leaves together and made coverings for themselves.

This is the first moment, as image-bearers of God, humankind misstepped and misrepresented God. This is a turning point, and there seems to be no way out for both Adam and the woman. Genesis 3:9–10 continues,

"But the LORD God called to the man, 'Where are you?' He answered, 'I heard you in the garden, and I was afraid because I was naked; so I hid.'"

The results of this watershed moment are immense. From that point on, our narratives and identities as God's royal representatives became festered with falsehoods, sin, and shame. Humanity's initial instinct was now to flee and hide from God's presence rather than walk in harmony.

> Humanity's initial instinct was now to flee and hide from God's presence rather than walk in harmony.

The story continues with God asking both the man and the woman what had happened. Adam blames God's gift to him, the woman, for the result of their actions. The woman blames the serpent.

So the LORD God said to the serpent: "Because you have done this, cursed are you above all livestock and all wild animals! You will crawl on your belly and you will eat dust all the days of your life. And I will put enmity between you and the woman, and between your offspring and hers; he will crush your head, and you will strike his heel." (vv. 14–15)

God decides to curse the serpent, but there are consequences for the woman and man as well. God continues by speaking to his creatures:

To the woman he said, "I will make your pains in childbearing very severe; with painful labor you will give birth to children. Your desire will be for your husband, and he will rule over you." To Adam he said, "Because you listened to your wife and ate fruit from the tree about which I commanded you, 'You must not eat from it,' cursed is the ground because of you; through painful toil you will eat food from it all the days of your life. It will produce thorns and thistles for you, and you will eat the plants of the field. By the sweat of your brow you will eat your food until you return to the ground, since from it you were taken; for dust you are and to dust you will return." (vv. 16–19)

When humankind adopted the serpent's alternative narrative, the ramifications were insurmountable. Adam and the woman tainted their image-bearing representation of God. Their functional purposes were now marred by their wrong actions.

While the woman was deceived, Adam willingly ate the fruit. Instead of ruling over the created world with ease, enjoyment, and creativity, their days became infiltrated with dysfunction. Their lives were consistently filled with sweat and toil, broken relationships, and pain. Survival, rather than a flourishing life, became the default mode of humanity.

At the end of Genesis 3, God creates new garments for Adam and his wife. The fig leaves didn't suffice for their lives. God banishes them—and their newfound knowledge of good and evil—from Eden. The angels take on the guardianship of the tree of life instead of humanity. That way, Adam and his wife don't eat from that as well and live forever in rampant dysfunction, sin, and shame.

The consequences of the downfall of Eden remain even now. Rather than things going easily, there are consistent problems to be solved. Death, toil, relational strife, sin, shame, and disconnection from God reign throughout our lives.

What are we to do?

We need a hero.

## Cultivating Curiosity

1. God placed his "image" and "likeness" in us. What does that mean to you when you understand it is about functionality and not the aesthetics?

2. What does your role seem to be in its pre-fall state in God's narrative?

3. What negative ways do you see people using God's instilled rulership in us? Look back at *kabash* and *radah*.

4. What would it look like for you to embellish your life with beauty (*shamar*)?

5. Is there any other alternative interpretation to Genesis 1–3 that has been pivotal to your understanding of who you are? If so, what is it?

# NOTES

# NOTES

# CHAPTER 5

# WHY IS IT IMPORTANT
# TO HAVE A HERO?

*Let us not forget that human knowledge and skills alone*
*cannot lead humanity to a happy and dignified life.*

—ALBERT EINSTEIN

W HY DO WE NEED A HERO?

I honestly think we should ask Marvel this question. But I don't have personal connections there. So we will go about seeking our answer from a researcher's perspective.

Why does Marvel think heroes have a place in saving the world? Truly, their superhero roster is stacked. Hulk, Spider Man, Doctor Strange, and Captain America are just a few names on Marvel's iconic roster. Each hero has a special origin story, along with special abilities to counteract evil.

Hulk was originally just a brilliant scientist named Dr. Bruce Banner. He was exposed to gamma radiation, which sometimes transformed him into Hulk—a large, green, anger-induced superhuman. His anger is a result of trauma induced by his father during childhood that is now used to save the world from various villains.[1]

Spider-Man was originally Peter Parker, a teenager who was bitten by a radioactive spider. He now splits his time between being nerdy Peter Parker and using his superhero Spidey-Sense abilities to save the world by fighting crime as your "friendly neighborhood Spider-Man."[2]

Doctor Strange was originally a renowned surgeon who suffered from a severe injury to both of his hands, cutting his career short. In searching for a cure, Stephen Strange looks for the Ancient One. He develops a third eye, becomes a magical martial arts guru, and protects the earth from the many mystical forces.[3]

Captain America was originally Steve Rogers, a WWII soldier. He went into the war a pretty normal—even scrawny—guy and came out as a Super Soldier. Transformed by Super-Soldier serum, he uses his nearly indestructible shield in battle. Interestingly, while he is the leader of the Avengers, he is actually one of the "most human" members of the Marvel hero world.[4]

No matter how strange the backstory of each hero, and no matter what tragedies they have experienced, we seem as a general public to agree with Marvel that we need heroes to help us defeat evil. At the time of this writing, Marvel is the largest franchise in movie history.[5]

While Marvel's superheroes have wild origin stories, impressive crime-fighting resumes, and worthy foes, none of these storylines come close to the origin story of Christ and his heroism.

## The Serpent and the Proclaimed Hope

As we wrestle with the ongoing painful results of the downfall of paradise, it's easy to forget that in God's statements to the serpent, the man, and the woman, there is profound hope.

When God told the woman that her seed would crush the serpent, this was the moment in which Adam first gave his wife a name, and he named her Eve to describe her new calling in life. The word he uses for Eve is *chava*, meaning "life" or "mother of the living." From her offspring would come One who would defeat the serpent and its schemes.[6]

There would be a Hero who would come to rescue humanity from its fallen state.

After Adam and Eve were banished from the garden, God was patient and allowed humanity to continue in their role as his royal representatives. In Genesis 6, our ruling methods became wicked. As the world's population grew, "every inclination of the thoughts of the human heart was only evil all the time" (v. 5). Humanity was exercising its power in a sinister way, opposite of God's desire for a world ruled with love and service.

God's people continued in their evil ways with their misaligned hearts and twisted lives. Things got so terrible during Jeremiah's time that God sent his people into exile and issued them a "certificate of divorce" (spoiler: God's not actually going to divorce them). Despite God's righteous anger, his mercy, love, and compassion prevailed. Afterward, God asked for his people to come back three times, even though they continued being unfaithful to him by worshiping false gods.

Even throughout all this adulterous behavior of God's people, God continued to speak to them through the law, prophets, and kings. Each passing generation received new prophecies and words of hope, but no Hero emerged.

The last proclamation came to the prophet Malachi. After God spoke to Malachi, there were over four hundred years of silence from God before he gave new revelation in the New Testament. There's not really an explanation for the silence; on the surface, it seems like God "ghosted" Israel.

During those four hundred years, I'm guessing that God's people had a hard time hanging onto hope. Hope might have felt too irrational, disappointing, and painful. While there are no books written in those years due to the prophetic silence, surely the Jews had questions about the God who proclaimed to love them:

"Doesn't God love us anymore?"

"We thought God was going to provide a Hero to save us from this fallen world filled with injustice and wickedness. Has he changed his mind?"

"Are we holding out hope for nothing?"

At the end of the four hundred years, Jesus finally arrived on the scene. The Hero came as a baby, born of the Virgin Mary. Talk about weird origin stories. There wasn't a radioactive spider bite or a superhero serum. God simply showed up as a helpless baby. This was different than what many had been hoping for.

Instead of arriving majestically and powerfully, the Hero's arrival was humble. Like Marvel's mythical origin stories, there's a lot that is unknown about Jesus until he turned thirty and began teaching with authority and proclaiming the hope of the kingdom. But what we see in his ministry is the God-Man living and ruling in the way God always intended for us: in love, service, and humility. He embodied *radah* as it was always intended—to go down, as equals, walking among the subjects and serve (like God did in the garden).

At the age of thirty-three, Jesus Christ became the "last Adam," overthrowing the reign of sin and death that the "first Adam" brought upon the world (1 Corinthians 15:45). We can see lots of foreshadowing and parallels between the story of Adam and of Christ. Both stories include the ideas of a garden, sweat, thorns, a tree, a curse, and death.

In Genesis, Adam lived in a garden, ate from the forbidden tree, and fell under a curse of sweat and toil as a result of sin brought into this world. From that point on, the fields would have thorns and work would be a challenge. Instead of eternal life, one would die.

Before Christ's death, he stopped in the garden of Gethsemane to pray. He was in such distress that he began to sweat blood. When he was arrested by the Roman soldiers, they mocked him and placed a crown of thorns on his head. Christ was murdered on a cross formed from a tree, making the one sacrifice for all, becoming the curse for us. Christ broke the curse of sin and death that reigned over humanity by being the ultimate sacrifice and conquering the grave.

By submitting to a horrific death, Christ fulfilled God's age-old promise of hope. The Hero who reigned with love showed up for all the world to take part in this redemptive event. In this event, Christ redefines human existence and inaugurates a new era filled with a slate of new opportunities for our relationship with God.

## What Does This Mean for Human Existence?

Christ's death and resurrection changed everything—and I do mean *everything*. His heroic feat of living a sinless life, sacrificing his life on the cross, and then resurrecting to defeat death is not just your average "saving the day" historic event. This is not just an inspirational story that someone can look to as a nice example of heroism.

This event inaugurated a new way of life. A new way of being.

When we believe in Christ as our Hero—or in traditional Christian language, our "Lord and Savior"—it changes one's life and initiates a new way of being, a new personal timeline.

This isn't accomplished through Marvel-esque means, like obtaining a third eye or being injected with serum. It happens when we accept Christ as our Hero and are "born again."

Jesus said, "Truly, truly, I say to you, unless one is born again he cannot see the kingdom of God" (John 3:3). When we are born again, we see the truth of Jesus Christ and the realities of the kingdom of God.

Christ has died.

Christ has risen.

Christ will come again.

> God's kingdom flips the script on what it means to live and rule: suffering, sorrow, humiliation, and service eclipse power and control.

In the meantime, we can be born again, living a new, victorious life in a supernatural kingdom that has yet to be fully realized on earth. This is our testament of faith. Suffering, victory, and hope all wrapped up into one.

What Christ accomplished through his life, death, and resurrection was revolutionary. God's kingdom flips the script on what it means to live and rule: suffering, sorrow, humiliation, and service eclipse power and control.

While God's demonstration of love was and still is revolutionary, it was just the beginning. Through this act, God did something even more unexpected. He made it possible to actually place himself in our hearts. By grace through faith, the Holy Spirit now resides in our hearts. Instead of a heart eclipsed by evil, we now have a heart enlightened by love. This miraculous prophecy was recorded in Ezekiel 36:26-27, which proclaims, "I will give you a new heart and put a new spirit in you; I will remove from you your heart of stone and give you a heart of flesh. And I will put my Spirit in you and move you to follow my decrees and be careful to keep my laws."

With this new heart and Spirit, we have newfound confidence and conviction of who we are. Here is just a small sampling of the truth that the Spirit speaks to us:

- We are both loved and adopted by God. (Romans 8:15; Galatians 4:6)
- With God as our Father, we no longer have to live in a spirit of slavery and fear. (Romans 8:15)
- We have access to power and boldness to witness to the testimony of Jesus. (1 Timothy 1:7–9)
- We have freedom through God's Spirit. (2 Corinthians 3:17)
- God's Spirit, which cannot lie, helps us know what is true about all things. (1 John 2:27)

- The Spirit grounds us and roots us in love so we can comprehend the love of Christ that surpasses knowledge. (Ephesians 3:19)
- The Spirit sets the seal of ownership on us as a deposit in our hearts, guaranteeing what is to come. (2 Corinthians 1:22; John 16:33)

When we receive the Holy Spirit and listen to what the Spirit wants to teach us, it answers once and for all the question: "Who am I, and why am I here?"

God knows that when the heart is changed, one's life is changed. We are not transformed by flipping through books of knowledge, or mere facts of a historical event. We are transformed by experiencing the love of God.

This love that surpasses any human understanding witnesses to us who we are, and to whom we belong. We are now a part of God's eternal family. This love bears witness to the grander story. We are embedded into the story of the gospel and Jesus' return, which we share wherever we go. This love ushers us into a paradigm-shifting kingdom story.

But if we are loved by God and have truth in our hearts now, why are things still hard, painful, and confusing? It's because we are in the "already-not yet" chapter of the kingdom story.

## What Does "Already–Not Yet" Mean?

As I've mentioned, we are influenced by the time and place in which we live, and you and I are living in the "already-not yet" part of God's grand story.

When theologians speak of already-not yet, they are speaking about the fact that God's kingdom is both present and futuristic. The kingdom of God is inaugurated and present, but it will not be realized in its full state until Christ comes again.

In this "time between times," there are things that remain in existence that will not remain in the future. Some of these include sin, shame, and suffering. These are brutal to experience, and they are here to stay until Christ returns.

No wonder we can be born again and have truth in our hearts, yet life can still be painful, hard, and confusing!

To put it simply, we are living and breathing already-not yet people. This is an often misunderstood and misinterpreted feature of Scripture. Dr. David Briones, a professor in New Testament, notes this about our current reality:

- *already* adopted in Christ (Romans 8:15), but *not yet* adopted (Romans 8:23)
- *already* redeemed in Christ (Ephesians 1:7), but *not yet* redeemed (Ephesians 4:30)
- *already* sanctified in Christ (1 Corinthians 1:2), but *not yet* sanctified (1 Thessalonians 5:23–24)
- *already* saved in Christ (Ephesians 2:8), but *not yet* saved (Romans 5:9)
- *already* raised with Christ (Ephesians 2:6), but *not yet* raised (1 Corinthians 15:52).[7]

These New Testament passages indicate we do indeed live in this already-not yet timeline. While we *already* are these things factually, sometimes we do *not yet* experience the fullness of this reality because we are not in that chapter of God's story yet.

While we live in this time, it is important we remain in this crucible and appreciate the tension. It is obvious there is plenty to celebrate about the present; and it is also obvious there is more to come in the future.

And herein lies our conundrum.

How do we embrace the chapter of God's story in which we find ourselves living?

How do we balance the already-not yet nature of our faith?

What does it mean to be an already-not yet image-bearer of God?

## Cultivating Curiosity

1.  Do you believe your role has changed in God's larger story since the fall? Why or why not?
2.  Christ is our Hero. Do you believe it is healthy or unhealthy to try to be a hero? Why or why not?
3.  Do you believe Christ's act—"suffering, sorrow, humiliation, and service eclipsing power and control"—is still relevant today?
4.  Take a look at what we receive from the Spirit. Which offerings speak most loudly to you and why?
5.  Do you believe the majority of Christians look through the already-not yet lens? If so, what is your evidence?

# NOTES

# NOTES

# CHAPTER 6

## WHY AM I JUST NOW FINDING OUT I'M IN A WAR?

*Life has its own hidden forces*
*which you can only discover by living.*

—SØREN KIERKEGAARD

What War?

Look, I'm a smaller individual who can't shoot a gun at anything, and my skills with a knife are limited to cutting fruits and vegetables. My most accurate form of aim is weaponizing a tennis racquet and a ball going approximately eighty-five miles per hour max, which is not exactly deadly.

When I heard we had a Hero, I assumed our work was over and that Christ would do it all. I imagined humanity's role was relatively passive and that our responsibilities were limited to being rescued—again, and again, and again.

I was incredibly wrong.

This whole already-not yet existence has a lot of plot twists I didn't fully understand. And I'll be honest about this one: I didn't necessarily like it. Partially because I didn't pass clearance to be recruited for the US Armed Forces, so I had no idea why I had a war on my hands, especially one that involved the kingdom of God.

It turns out we have had a war declared on us simply due to the fact that we live in this timeline. Both sin and Satan have declared a war on each of us; it's just a matter of you deciding to do anything about it or not. Let's look at the first culprit: sin.

Sin is a pretty savage beast. In fact, Scripture describes sin in a hunting, fishing, and predatory type of language. Sin is *crouching at the door, a lure, enticing and drags us away.*

The first time sin is formally named is in Genesis 4:7: "If you do what is right, will you not be accepted? But if you do not do what is right, sin is crouching at your door; it desires to have you, but you must rule over it."

Think it is a coincidence that sin's first description directly challenges humanity's primary call as royal ruling image-bearers? Absolutely not. Sin's desire is to rule you; it wants to be the fiercest force in your life. Sin's goal is to be the author of your master narrative. It desires to control your beliefs, thoughts, values, and behaviors.

Sin's rulership is not portrayed in a royal, godlike *radah* fashion—with service, love, and humility in mind. It comes from a tyrannical mindset, not a benevolent king. Its goal is to take you captive, not set you free.

While our image-bearing representation has been clarified by Christ's rule and redemption, sin and Satan want to overthrow the narrative of God's love, truth, and sacrifice. As we are being conformed to the image of Christ, sin's voice is still active, present, and desires all the attention.

When sin and Satan gets their way, evil gets its way. Here are a few things that result: murder, adultery, theft, and slander. When evil has its way, not only do you personally suffer as a result, but so does your community and relationship with God.

I learned long ago on a tennis court that it is good to study your opponent. Studying the opponent permits us to see both their strengths and their weaknesses. It gives us greater awareness of how they work, which allows us to understand how we should work and respond.

## Sin and Satan's Tactics: Good Positioning and Misplaced Desire

While Adam and Eve had a little advantage of sin being *outside* them, sin is now *inside* us. Theologically, this is most often called our "sin nature." There is a natural propensity inside each of us to believe and behave in a way contrary to God.

Sin also sits at the core of who we are—our hearts. It is centered in the crux of our being. In this already-not yet world, our sinful nature never completely leaves us. We have been infiltrated for eons. It is an ever-present reality. The very nature of our lives is not a neutral playing ground.

> The very nature of our lives is not a neutral playing ground.

While we cannot shift its position or presence, we can know its strategies. When sin or Satan make a move, it is not necessarily a surprise. The plays are good but also predictable. It all begins with desire. Desire in and of itself isn't bad. God created you with desires, wants, needs, and interdependence. Each of us have needs outside ourselves that are best met through our relationships with others and with God. Sin and the plays of Satan simply capitalize on already existing desires and then pervert them.

Since the fall of humanity, our intimacy with God has been distorted by sin. Our desires, wants, and interdependence have been perverted in a way that is contrary to how God created us. Understanding which desires are good and bad is the challenging part.

When we begin to feel this tug toward sin, we are entering temptation territory. Temptation in and of itself is not a sin. Every person lives with it. What matters is whether you follow through with the temptation. Here are some ways that you'll likely be lured in:

**Temptation appeals to our senses and our desire for pleasure**. Temptation can present itself through manipulation, seduction, or simply considering gluttonous behavior. Its lure will tap into your sensual desires, whether that be through taste, touch, smell, or even imagination. Some temporal pleasures that have the potential to turn into sin include food, sex, power, money, or work.

**Temptation distracts us from thinking about the consequences**. When you feel tempted to do something you know is wrong—stealing, drinking, having sex in the wrong context, and so on—you're focused on the pleasure, not the consequences. For example, you're thinking about the thrill of walking out the store doors with that watch under your jacket; you're not thinking about getting caught. You're focused on the pleasure of that next drink; you're not thinking about the drive home or a potential DUI. You're fantasizing about intimate moments with that person you just met; you're not thinking about STDs, unwanted pregnancies, or even the emotional wounds of sex outside of marriage.

**Temptation offers expedient solutions to your problems**. The solutions that temptation promises resemble those of infomercials that are too good to be true. That stolen watch will make you feel regal instead of insignificant. That next drink will solve your social anxiety. That one-night stand could be your ticket to lasting love and an end to your loneliness.

Temptation wears all kinds of masks and disguises so that we are lured and dragged away into a life full of disaster. Temptation has the capacity to lead to sin, which ultimately leads to death. Temptation by itself isn't wrong, nor is it sin. We are all tempted by Satan and our own thoughts and desires. The problem isn't that a wrong or dangerous thought enters your mind; it's when you invite it to hang around. Temptation has been described as a bird flying over our head—it's going to happen. The problem starts when we invite it to make a nest in our hair.

## When We Give in to Temptation, What Happens?

We are both sinful by nature and by choice. Temptation, when given the chance to take ground, progresses into sin. And sin always leads to death.

**Sin dehumanizes humanity**. God created humanity sinless, and anything less than that isn't the Creator's desire or design. Sin steals our God-given humanity, and instead makes us inhumane. Sin does not produce a world filled with beauty, creativity, and things that flourish. Sin leads to a life filled with brutality, mundanity, and failure.

"Good things grow" is a common saying. But the opposite is also true: bad things grow. Sin can begin as a small pleasure that you enjoy. It can easily graduate into a habit that costs you time and money. Sin can then transform into a prison that takes you captive and be the only reason for your existence because you believe it is where true life is found.

**Sin corrupts our relationships**. In the first story of sin with Adam and Eve, harmony and bliss were no more. It corrupted their relationships with both one another and God. Adam and Eve both hid from God. Adam blamed Eve.

Instead of taking on personal responsibility for our actions, we continue to blame and hide as they did. But we do even more: we gossip about people we hang out with, creating distrust. We become jealous of others' accomplishments instead of being proud. We don't appreciate other people's beauty. Instead, we need to become better. Sin causes division and disconnection.

**Sin influences our choice of friends and larger community**. Some friendships have their foundation in sin. It can be initiated by one person and then be imitated by others easily. Sin has the capacity to magnify greatly. Our sinful nature produces lives filled with gossip, slander, evil thoughts, and deeds instead of harmony, beauty, creativity and appreciation.

If sin is the basis of some friendships, it can also be the basis of some societies or business ventures. Sin can be the fabric that connects social groups, cultures, and institutions. The web of stories sin produces is wrapped in deceit, deception, and death.

**Sin fuels oppression.** Sin gives us an improper view of ourselves. It is often filled with complete arrogance and pride—and in that name, disregarding the value of others. Comparison is often looked upon so innocently. But it's anything but innocent. If one person is inherently better than the other based on birth, social status, beauty, or whatever "criteria of comparison," then we just devalued a person made in the image of God. That's the beginning of oppression.

In Amos 2:6–7 it speaks of Israel's sin in this way: "They sell the righteous for silver, and the needy for a pair of sandals. They trample on the heads of the poor as upon the dust of the ground and deny justice to the oppressed." Sin isn't just denying others' needs or justice. In this action, it is decimating the love of God.

**Sin deceives us into thinking we're doing the right thing when we're not.** Finally, sin can be so deceptive, it convinces people they are doing the right thing. In Isaiah 5:20 it says, "Woe to those who call evil good and good evil, who put darkness for light and light for darkness, who put bitter for sweet and sweet for bitter."

The world can convince itself that it is doing good, but in fact evil is being manifested. The religious leaders of the day crucified the Creator of the world. With sincerity in their hearts, they believed it not only right but an act of worship to crucify the "friend of sinners."

The power of sin is very grand. Its power lies in its invisibility, like other master narratives. Then it spreads into mass misinformation. It steals our life.

The good news is, sin doesn't have to overtake us; it can stay in the temptation phase. In 1 Corinthians 10:13 it says, "No temptation has overtaken you that is not common to man. God is faithful, and he will not let you be tempted beyond your ability, but with the temptation he will also provide the way of escape, that you may be able to endure it." Let's learn how to fight back.

## How Do We Fight Back?

Sure, we are never on a neutral playing field. Temptation is ever-present, lurking both within and outside us. But the Spirit and sin reside in the same place. We don't need to be afraid, "For he who is greater in us than he who is in the world" (1 John 4:4). We just need to learn what our abilities are to counteract these two forces.

**Normalize temptation**. It can be tempting as Christians to want to only talk about the glorious progress of their faith. We are, in fact, a new creation. But that dismisses the tension of already not yet. This would be a grave mistake for sin or Satan to win the day.

We need to normalize being tempted toward sin and discuss it with both God and each other. Satan would love for us to think that we should keep our sinful thoughts to ourselves because we are ashamed and should be "past it."

James 1:13 says, "when tempted." We should be alert and accept the reality that exists. Becoming like Christ is not a ticket out of temptation. Transforming into Christ means choosing righteousness over sin every day.

This is an ongoing and normal process for every person. 1 John 1:8–9 says, "If we claim to be without sin, we deceive ourselves and the truth is not in us. If we confess our sins, he is faithful and just and will forgive us our sins and purify us from all unrighteousness." Let us not be prideful in our new nature and accept we still struggle on this side of eternity.

**Deserting or fleeing is a worthy option in battle**. While deserting might be a disgrace in the military, it is a worthy tactic in the God's kingdom battles. In 2 Timothy 2:22 it says, "Flee the evil desires of youth and pursue righteousness, faith, love and peace, along with those who call on the Lord out of a pure heart."

We do not only flee, though. When we are fleeing, we are actively pursuing something else. We must pursue "righteousness, faith, love and peace." The idea is to leave one desire and fuel them with another because of how our minds work. Our thoughts are meant to dwell on things. Simply saying, "Stop sinning!" is not a worthy tactic to defeat temptation. The way we fight temptation is to create new neural pathways in our brain and form a new kind of story. We redirect our devotion toward God and the unfolding kingdom story.

We can decide to dwell on truth, or we can dwell on temptation. Let's normalize what we dwell on and fight back. When we flee, we are actively redirecting toward a faith-paved path.

> We can decide to dwell on truth, or we can dwell on temptation.

**Take note of your temptation pattern and make a plan**. Not everyone is tempted the same way. Some struggle with gluttony, others with gossip. There is a wide range for us to be enticed. The temptation you face is always tailored to you. Otherwise, it wouldn't be so alluring.

Once you've lived for a while and thought about your life, you'll notice you have patterns of thoughts and actions. There is correlation between the two of these. Your thoughts carry you places.

It is important to notice common factors (places and people) when you are tempted. Where will you be? Who will you be with? Are you alone? What are you thinking and doing? After you have noticed the pattern, make a plan. It can be simple. Or it can be elaborate, depending upon the circumstance.

If you ever intentionally hide, conceal, or are alone when leaning toward temptations, this is a warning sign that needs attention. Proverbs 18:1 says, "Whoever isolates himself seeks his own desire; he breaks out against all sound judgment." Darkness and selfish desires have taken over. Inviting others in is necessary to win the battle.

If you're with other people, then preparations are in order. Are you strong enough for the temptation ahead? Is it best to not go? Who will be there that will be a support or drag you down? Do you need a Christian friend to call at a certain point in the night? What are the options to pursue righteousness and not sin?

**Resist the devil by knowing the Word of God.** God has given us his Spirit within our very hearts, and that's amazing. But we don't get a transplant of God's Word already written on our hearts. We're required to do the work of memorization to learn our loving Narrator's words.

With every temptation Satan threw at Jesus, he quoted Scripture in return. Satan knows Scripture, so I wouldn't suggest arguing with Satan over its meaning and application. I suggest learning the meaning and application with others and in your time alone.

Not memorizing Scripture is not adequately preparing yourself for battle. God's grace is abundant. But let's not use grace as a license to do nothing.

**Always ask for God's help**. Prayer is not a secondhand weapon. Being on your knees isn't a sign of surrender in the kingdom of God. Being on your knees is debatably the most powerful position.

God says, "Call upon me in the day of trouble; I will deliver you, and you shall glorify me" (Psalm 50:15). Dependence on God is not a weakness. It is an act of faith that brings glory to God. Your prayers can act as a testimony of faith.

We can approach God confidently in our time of need. Hebrews 4:15–16 says, "For we do not have a high priest who is unable to empathize with our weaknesses, but we have one who has been tempted in every way, just as we are—yet he did not sin. Let us then approach God's throne of grace with confidence, so that we may receive mercy and find grace to help us in our time of need." God is for you, for righteousness, and for his glory. In desperation, we can boldly approach him.

As Christians, we fight differently because we are, in fact, different. Our weapons may seem peculiar or our methods odd, but they are not less effective. In fact, they are better than any weapon in the present. Ephesians 1:18–21 says, "I pray that the eyes of your heart may be enlightened in order that you may know the hope to which he has called you, the riches of his glorious inheritance in his holy people, and his incomparably great power for us who believe. That power is the same as the mighty strength he exerted when he raised Christ from the dead and seated him at his right hand in the heavenly realms, far above all rule and authority, power and dominion, and every name that is invoked, not only in the present age but also in the one to come."

Power in these verses is the Greek word *dunamis*, which is where we get the word *dynamite*. Its most common translation is "power, ability, and strength." This tells us that in believing in Christ as Lord, with the power and indwelling of the Holy Spirit, we do have the God-given ability, power, and strength to resist any evil thrown our way. We now can fight (and win) battles that we were not previously equipped to fight.[1]

Sin and Satan, while powerful in their own ways, are no match for the *dunamis* that lives in us. We will need this power for another equally vile evil we must contend with in our life that gets between us, God, and our relationships that we will explore in the next chapter.

## Cultivating Curiosity

1. The first description of sin likens it to a ruler. In what ways can sin become your master narrative instead of God's kingdom story? How would your purpose in life change if sin was your master instead of God?

2. In which ways are you most commonly tempted?

3. How are you currently fighting sin?

4. Create an escape plan for yourself if you have a repetitive sin.

5. Many people don't know how to practice accountability with one another. Do you have any ideas on how to assist in resolving that?

# NOTES

# NOTES

# CHAPTER 7

WHAT DOES NEW YEAR'S HAVE
TO DO WITH ANYTHING?

*Shame corrodes the very part of us that believes we are*
*capable of change.*

—BRENÉ BROWN

ONE OF MY FAVORITE TIMES OF THE YEAR IS NEW YEAR'S EVE.
I have my own special tradition in which I look back at the past
year, reflect on my present, and look forward to the future. Every
year it's the same story: I get to relive (and anticipate!) amazing
triumphs, downfalls, mundaneness, and all that's in between.

And while I have my own New Year's tradition, one
tradition that I never intend to adopt is to set a New Year's
resolution. "New year! New me!" is not my cup of tea. But for
those who do participate in New Year's resolutions, it is also
often the same story year after year.

Plans typically involve changing oneself for the better—
perhaps losing weight, eating healthier, or feeling happier.

Sometimes they encompass financial gain, relational stability, or healing from past trauma.

In all my years, I have never heard of any resolution list including the following:

1. I want to learn how to be angrier so my relationships can improve.
2. I'd like to learn the art of being more selfish to make life more fulfilling.
3. I need to learn to become better at procrastinating at all my life's dreams and ambitions.

These goals, while humorous, are never going to make the list. No one needs a plan to be better at these things—unfortunately, they come as naturally as breathing.

Why, though?

Things like anger, selfishness, and procrastination come naturally because we are sinful beings. It goes back to the downfall of Eden and the already-not yet narrative. The result of this storyline is that while we long for transformation, sometimes we feel stuck. Feeling stuck—and our longing to experience positive change—is the reason every year we vow to realize these changes in our life despite the fact that we keep falling short.

One of the big reasons we are stuck has to do with shame.

Brené Brown has become the shame guru in recent years, and she defines shame as this: "Shame is the fear of disconnection . . . Shame is the intensely painful feeling or experience of believing that we are flawed and therefore unworthy of love, belonging, and connection."[1] Shame directly challenges the good news of the gospel: that God loves the world so much, his son died on a cross so we shall not perish but have everlasting life.

In Christ, we have love, belonging, and connection eternally. This is no coincidence. Christ's death on the cross is linked with overcoming shame. Hebrews 12:2 explains: "For the joy that was set before him, he endured the cross, despising the shame." This includes the shame of death by the cross, which was associated with the worst criminal acts, as well as the shame of the fall, which humanity has carried ever since Adam and Eve's choice in the garden.

We know that the fall of mankind in the garden of Eden is the turning point because the *absence of shame* is one of the last things mentioned about humanity before the whole fruit fiasco. Genesis 2:25 says, "Adam and his wife were both naked, and they felt no shame."

I have always been curious about this passage. Not only because it is the beginning of our master narrative, but because it is interesting what the author of Genesis decides to say (or not say, for that matter). Why didn't the author mention that Adam and Eve felt loved? Or comfortable? Or happy or successful or safe?

Instead, the author says they felt no shame.

I don't believe it is a mistake or a misprint. I believe it is because shame is a key element to the human condition. Curt Thompson, a Christian psychiatrist, puts shame in an even clearer light:

> Shame is not just a consequence of something our first parents did in the Garden of Eden. It is the emotional

weapon that evil uses to (1) corrupt our relationships with God and each other and (2) disintegrate any and all gifts of vocational vision and creativity . . . It is both a source and result of evil's active assault on God's creation, and a way for evil to try to hold out until the new heavens and earth appear at the consummation of history.[2]

To be human in this already-not yet world is to deal both with sinful desires and the voices of shame. Both are unrelenting in their presence in our lives. In light of shame's pivotal role, we need to study the evil that exists so we can fight against it.

## What's Shame's Game?

Shame's game is stealthy. Both Brené and Curt demonstrate one of shame's most lethal features: it is emotive. Its power lies in the fact that it is first *felt*. Shame is a prelude to vocabulary. And when we do manage to put words to the feelings, the statements are piercing. Shame is typically expressed in "I am" statements that attack our core identity.

Common phrases include:

*I am not enough.*

*I am unlovable.*

*I am bad.*

Shame's narrative for your life directly contradicts our loving Narrator. God has declared that you are royal, redeemed and righteous. Meanwhile, shame insists on spewing stories of accusation, judgment, and condemnation.

A lot of people confuse shame and guilt. Let's take a quick look at the distinctions.

Guilt says, "I did something wrong."

Guilt is behavior-focused not identity-focused. In my culture (and others), there are numerous ways a person can move on from guilt. There are standard procedures, such as paying a fine, doing community service, or even serving jail time. Sometimes, for relational offenses, all one has to do is acknowledge they did something wrong, promise to not repeat the offense, and continue on.

While having a guilty conscience is never a pleasant experience, its outcomes are associated with goodness or change. We can apologize and/or make amends to move past what we have done.

Shame is altogether different.

Shame says, "There is something wrong with me."

Shame is identity-focused. Shame's accusation doesn't have a path or process back to wholeness and freedom. When faced with shame, we often cower, grimace, and allow it to become our master.

Unlike guilt, shame doesn't come with positive behavior outcomes. Instead, shame is so deep-seated and visceral that our responses to it can include addiction, bullying, depression, and violence. Having destructive responses and feeling stuck is only the beginning of shame's game. The ramifications are so much more.

**Shame puts our bodies in survival mode.** Shame is a protective emotion by nature. It puts our bodies on high alert as if there were an actual physical threat. Our bodies are expecting an attack, and the body responds with its three options: fight, flight, or freeze.

When our bodies are in this state, our higher cognitive thinking is off. This means our bodies are in response mode. Some people fight with their fists or their words, whether the attack is physical or emotional abuse. Others might flee when in a life-threatening situation. When we are in freeze mode, it is often when unspeakable things are happening to us.

Staying in this fear-infused state for long is not good. People who have been through traumatic events (whether repeated abuse, or military-related missions) have signs of PTSD and other psychological problems.

**Shame acts like an ongoing purgatory**. Brené Brown calls shame the "master emotion" because when shame rears its ugly head, all other emotions shut down. And it is an intensely painful feeling. In fact, Brown notes that current neuroscience suggests that the emotional pain caused by shame is just as real as physical pain.[3]

And that's not the only bad news. Shame tends to create more shame. It is a cyclical emotion. Whatever emotion we experience on an ongoing basis creates neural paths in our brain. Imagine these like wagon wheel ruts; they are easy to fall into over and over again, deepening each time we take that path.

**Shame keeps you from approaching God**. When Adam and Eve hid from God for the first time, it was because of shame. Shame acts as a blockade from God's love.

I often wonder what tone God used when he asked Adam, "Where are you?" When I read those words, I don't hear accusations or condemnation. I hear someone wanting to listen.

But shame makes the idea of being visible unbearable. We just want to cover up and isolate ourselves. We cannot imagine being seen and risking feeling judged.

If you have ever felt like you need to clean yourself up before you approach God, know you have moved from guilt to shame. Shame stifles your desire to be seen and known by God.

**Shame disconnects you from others**. Shame not only motivates us to hide from God, it also drives us to hide from each other. Once again, we want to avoid feeling accused or judged.

We may also hide because we feel that we don't deserve the comfort and intimacy that comes with being seen and known by others. Shame can even stop friendships from getting started. Shame says, *Why would this person like me?* And then you push someone away, or never allow the friendship to develop in the first place.

Sometimes we don't hide but move into attack mode. Shame can be expressed as rage, abusive behavior, projection, and blame. We see some of this when Adam blames Eve and God for what happened in the garden: "The man said, 'The woman you put here with me—she gave me some fruit from the tree, and I ate it'" (Genesis 3:12).

Shame creates a hostile environment between others. Shame is often rampant in places of marginalization of any kind (racism, sexism, etc.). It is set aflame by the disconnection and is kept burning by fear, distrust, and even hatred.

**Shame kills your vision and creativity**. When shame puts you in a state of emotional survival, your brain isn't in a state of futuristic thinking or creativity. Your cognitive energy is too focused on coping with the emotional pain to draw from other areas of the brain. In fact, the shame-fueled mind can be in a fog.

However, the fog of shame isn't voiceless. It continuously repeats things like:

*I suck.*

*I'll never be good enough.*

*My opinions don't matter.*

Shame is a disempowering emotion. It is a confidence-killer. Not only is it associated with low confidence; it can lead to self-sabotaging behaviors, including eating disorders, among many other crippling things.

When we are talking about both vision and creativity in your life, it is necessary to see a possible future and the potential in what is not yet seen. Whether that is imagining creating a new recipe, imagining your to-do list for the day or week ahead, or even attending a concert. You have to see your future *doing something.*

For these reasons and more, shame robs you of your vision for a successful, happy future. We must learn to combat this insidious and painful existence to step into the new life Christ offers.

## How Do We Fight Shame?

Fighting shame is much like fighting sin in this already-not yet world; it will continue to be a beastly battle until our last

> Defeating shame is both an art and a science.

breath. This fight has some distinctive aspects though.

Facing shame is facing an emotional stain, the shrewdness of which resembles that of the serpent. Shame is crafty and shape-shifts. Defeating shame is both an art and a science.

In order to face shame, we must revisit its definition because herein lies our answer. Shame is ultimately the fear of *disconnection*. Therefore, in order to get rid of shame, we must form a *reconnection*.

Fighting shame isn't a solo operation. While shame is primarily about oneself and is a self-conscious emotion by nature, it is always in response to a real or perceived judgment or disconnection between yourself and another. Destroying the evil weaponry of shame takes teamwork. We must reconnect. We must be loved and known in a non-accusatory way.

Reconnecting in a way that allows the healing of our shame requires two things: vulnerability and empathy. While this sounds simple, it is not. As a general rule, to be vulnerable is a challenge. Curt Thompson says this about vulnerability: "To feel vulnerable is to feel, as Adam and Eve did in their fruit fest, naked and ashamed."[4]

And not only must we face our shame, but we must be met with empathy, which, to be honest, is lacking in our society. Brené Brown writes, "Empathy is not about connecting to the experience, it is about connecting to the emotions that underpin the experience."[5] Let's take a closer look at the two things we need to experience freedom from our shame.

## What Does Vulnerability Look Like?

To heal from shame is an incredibly courageous act. While shame tells us to hide or become invisible, that is not how the pain of shame is healed. We must expose the shame to have a chance at the healing process.

Shame is similar to sin in this way. Confessing sin and bringing it to the light is a necessary component to defeating it. We must do the same with shame. Shame loves to control what we decide to share about ourselves. Secrets are its weapon of choice. Shame says, "I can love this part of my story. But not this part. It is too much, too terrible, too embarrassing. No one can ever know that."

Shame loves a life filled with secrets. But the secrets we keep only magnify the pain and reiterate the shame. It is like a nightshade plant; it grows in the dark. We must express the parts of ourselves that we believe are unlovable, terrible, and humiliating. Of course, we can always weep and be welcomed in the loving and secure presence of God. We can speak our shame, being held, healed, and covered by God's compassion. But more often than not, God allows another person to step in and aid in the healing process. We must dare to share, even at the risk of rejection.

It is noteworthy to mention that when being vulnerable, there is always the possibility of being shamed again. But being vulnerable is the only way to heal shame. We must take this daring leap so that we can be set free from the shackles of shame.

## Where Can I Find Empathy?

So where can I find this precious elixir that, when combined with vulnerability, cures shame? On one hand, it's really simple: we get empathy when we connect with people who know how to be empathetic.

What's *not* so simple is finding people with this skill. Empathy is in short supply and high demand. The reasons for this are many, but I believe that one reason is that empathy is not taught in school. Instead, our educational system relies on standardized tests to evaluate performance. This, in turn, makes us really good at comparison, judgment, and rejection. Our shame game is strong and rampant. Our empathy game is not.

As you are looking for someone who understands the power of empathy, here are some important things to consider. Look for these things:

**Someone who practices vulnerability with you.** If you have a friend who has never exposed their unwanted feelings of judgment and condemnation, it may be because vulnerability frightens them. Perhaps they have yet to discover how to face and address the voice of their own inner critic. If this is the case, they definitely won't know what to do with yours! No matter the cause, this is not the person for you because they won't know how to respond with empathy to your vulnerability. While it is ironic, when vulnerability is met with reciprocation, it heals. Our wounds heal the wounds of others. We mirror one another. Our words, eyes, and body language can say, "Me too!" Vulnerability breeds vulnerability.

**Someone who doesn't have a habit of gossiping.** If a friend is always telling you about the deepest and darkest secrets of other people, this is not the person who can provide for you a "safe place" or social security. This is a relationship red flag. This person isn't safe with anyone. In fact, being vulnerable with the wrong person can turn into a vicious cycle of abusing your trust and reinforcing your feelings of shame.

Particularly at the beginning of your journey toward healing, you are more delicate. While eventually, as you heal, your experience with shame may be shared in the public square, let it be at your own volition and not that of gossipers.

**Someone who is gifted in the art of listening.** Some people are fixated on fixing people. They like to be looked upon as experts, and perhaps in some areas of life they are. But dishing out advice and looking at people as projects and problems to be resolved does not help relieve shame. Instead, the way to provide a healing balm to someone who is suffering is to learn how to listen empathetically to the visceral pain of their shame.

A good listener can be found in a support group, or among your friends, family, mentors, or coaches. A person does not need the title of "counselor" to be a good listener. A title does not limit what a person has to offer—nor does it provide any kind of guarantee. What matters is whether or not they know how to practice the art of being empathetic.

When someone knows how to practice empathy, they recognize the power of mirroring another person's emotions. Empathy says, *I will sit in this emotional exposure with you. I will sit in your pain, and I will love you through it.*

Whatever the origins of your shame, there is hope. You do not have to remain stuck in cycles of shame. Our Hero has provided a path and process to restoration and wholeness through himself and others.

## Cultivating Curiosity

1.　How does shame inform your identity? What does shame suggest you do when it is your life's master?

2. How do you now understand the difference between shame and guilt?
3. In what incidences can shame and sin can be separated? Do you believe separating the two is even possible?
4. How can you practice empathy in specific situations?
5. What are ways we can incorporate vulnerability and empathy into our society to make it healthier?

# NOTES

# NOTES

# CHAPTER 8

# WAIT!
# SUFFERING AND REDEMPTION
# GO HAND IN HAND?

*We cannot wish old feelings away nor do spiritual exercises*
*for overcoming them until we have woven a healing story*
*that transforms our previous life's experience and gives*
*meaning to whatever pain we have endured.*

—JOAN BORYSENKO

SUFFERING IS A GUARANTEED PART OF HUMAN EXISTENCE.
We all have issues. They can range from mild frustrations to lifelong challenges. Suffering can manifest itself in minor inconveniences or problems throughout the day. But no matter who you are or where you live, even in the most paradise-like environments, suffering exists.

Probably the greatest plot twist of the already-not yet narrative is that not only does suffering exist, but it is not to be separated from redemption. As Christians, we hold suffering in one hand and redemption in the other.

Unfortunately, we haven't done such a good job of holding these tensions well. Over the years—at least in Western society—we have dismissed many great "normal" or less-chaotic testimonies for the flare of the before-and-after reveal. We like our home-improvement shows with their dramatic before-and-after reveals. We like radical transformation. We like stories of drug addicts who became pastors. The gluttonous person becomes a fitness fanatic.

And there's some good in that. I like a story about healing as good as the next person. But something that can get overlooked is the biblical narrative around suffering. While some suggest that an invitation to follow Jesus promises a one-way ticket to heaven and a prosperity-filled life, this is anything but accurate.

> **Prosperity is deceptive to the human heart.**

Prosperity is deceptive to the human heart. Following Jesus is neither a detour from pain nor a highway to a carefree life. If anything, following Christ guarantees trouble. 2 Timothy 3:12 says it plainly: "In fact, everyone who wants to live a godly life in Christ Jesus will be persecuted."

This very verse suggests that "good" and "bad" go hand in hand.

This suffering is not without significance though. Christian suffering actually puts us on a path that leads to good things and to blessings. Most importantly, it leads to transformation in ways that nothing else can.

This is why, surprisingly, the Bible tells us to *rejoice* in our sufferings. Rejoice? What a counterintuitive response to suffering! One passage that talks about suffering in this unexpected manner can be found in Romans 5:3–5.

"Not only that, but we rejoice in our sufferings, knowing that suffering produces endurance, and endurance produces character, and character produces hope, and hope does not put us to shame, because God's love has been poured into our hearts through the Holy Spirit who has been given to us."

This verse explores four important stepping-stones along this journey—suffering, endurance, character, and hope—that will allow us not only to survive but to rejoice even in the midst of challenges.

Let's take a look at each of these:

## Suffering

There is so much to be said about suffering. But for us, and the role it plays in our lives, it is necessary to grasp three key truths.

**Suffering isn't an indication of your standing with God.** Suffering doesn't mean you've messed up or are somehow less holy than someone who isn't suffering right now. Your life's circumstance—whether prison cell or mansion—is not evidence of your good standing with God.

In my own health journey, it has been suggested to me that I do not have "enough faith." I have been asked if there are any past sins of my ancestors that would suggest I deserved this infliction. I have even been told (in a kind way) that the source of my suffering isn't "demonically inflicted." I have been told some strange things and felt both judged and shamed, if I'm honest.

But health and materialistic blessings are not the equivalent of God's good favor. God's good character—or our good standing—is never on the altar for any of life's circumstances. In fact, if anything, the challenges we have provide assurance that we are God's people. 1 Peter 4:12 says, "Dear friends, do not be surprised at the fiery ordeal that has come on you to test you, as though something strange were happening to you." Possibly the most challenging part of this already-not yet narrative to swallow is that while we are lavished in love, this does not shield us from suffering. This confirms our place in the story.

**Suffering is an often-untapped resource of power**. Unless masochism is your ally, pain is mostly thought of as cringe-worthy. And that is an adequate response; pain is not something that is meant to be in this world. God's response to this visceral discomfort is pretty unexpected.

God decides to display his power in what we naturally believe to be powerless. Paul describes his ongoing source of pain in 2 Corinthians 12: 6–8 "I was given a thorn in my flesh, a messenger of Satan, to torment me. Three times I pleaded with the Lord to take it away from me. But he said to me, 'My grace is sufficient for you, for my power is made perfect in weakness.'"

Apparently—no matter if it's Satan or God—God can use our weakness to demonstrate his perfect power. For the man who wrote most of the New Testament, Paul made quite a statement. If God's power is made perfect in our weakness, then suffering is not a disadvantage in the kingdom of God. If anything, it is an advantage.

In light of this, we can genuinely embrace Paul's perspective in 2 Corinthians 12:9–11: "Therefore I will boast all the more gladly about my weaknesses, so that Christ's power may rest on me. That is why, for Christ's sake, I delight in weaknesses, in insults, in hardships, in persecutions, in difficulties. For when I am weak, then I am strong." Paul's words are the epitome of a pep talk. Since God makes our vulnerability his victory, we truly have nothing to lose. We can strut confidently in our shortcomings while the world cowers in shame.

**Suffering holds the space for some of our most sacred moments**. There is nothing that brings us to our knees more than the difficulties of life. When we are down and out, we do not have an expedient reservoir of resources to draw from. Our prayers are honest. Even if they are short, absent of words, and full of tears.

God chooses to be close to you in your most vulnerable, broken spaces. Psalm 34:18 says, "The LORD is close to the brokenhearted and saves those who are crushed in spirit." God is with the down-and-out and is unafraid of your brokenness. God is more than capable of sitting alongside you in the silence of your pain. From God's presence in Eden, to Christ coming and being named Immanuel (God with us), to the Holy Spirit dwelling in us—God is completely and totally with us.

Isaiah 53:3 says this of Christ: "He was despised and rejected by mankind, a man of suffering, and familiar with pain." It is not just the pain on the cross; it's the pain of the entire human lifespan. Simply because our world might not have the right language or empathy skills for suffering does not deny its importance. Christ didn't get the title "Man of Sorrows" to despise it; instead, this title is to confirm its sacred space in our life.

## Endurance

While suffering in and of itself isn't glamorous, endurance doesn't necessarily look any prettier. In fact, endurance is a painful process that requires perspective to ensure success.

**Endurance is painful.** Endurance is not a glamorous gig. If anything, it is a gritty one. Before the fall of humankind, there was no evidence that suggested work entailed frustration, sweat, and toil. Even after being forgiven by God, pain remains inevitable.

You're not obliged to evade your painful feelings or dismiss the fact that suffering is hard. Hebrews 12:11 says, "No discipline seems pleasant at the time, but painful."

**Endurance is a process.** Enduring through difficulty is not a one-time event. In other translations, endurance is equated with perseverance or patience. It literally means to "abide under or remain under."[1]

Sometimes patience can be perceived as passivity. But *how you wait* is not absent of thought or action. For example, if you live an average life expectancy, you'll spend five years in line, whether that's at the store, at traffic lights, or at an amusement park.[2] We all know we are indeed doing *something* while practicing patience at a traffic light, grocery shopping, or waiting for any government-provided service (even if it is sitting in frustration).

Perseverance is also not passive. It requires time, and it requires that you sweat and grind. Muscles develop over time when pressure is repeatedly applied. It is this idea of a continual, ongoing state of persistence, likened to a marathon runner rather than a sprinter.

**Endurance changes our perspective**. Lastly, perseverance changes our perspective. Looking beyond the pain is a key component of enduring. In Hebrews 12:11 it says that "it produces a harvest of righteousness and peace for those who have been trained by it." Endurance is training for greater gains.

1 Peter 4:13–14 expands on this: "Rejoice inasmuch as you participate in the sufferings of Christ, so that you may be overjoyed when his glory is revealed. If you are insulted because of the name of Christ, you are blessed, for the Spirit of glory and of God rests on you." We can increase our endurance by tapping into the truth that we are united with Christ and his eternal glory.

Finally, we can fix our focus on Jesus as the perfect example of our faith. Just as he looked at the joy ahead to endure the cross, so we can shift our perspective. Looking forward to future joy aids us in not growing weary in the process.

## Character

After undergoing the process of suffering and endurance, one's character comes to light. This is comparable to a character in your favorite novel or movie. As the plot develops and the character undergoes different challenges, you get to know more of their personality quirks, demeanor, and overall personhood.

**Character is revealed through suffering and endurance**. The Greek word here for character is *dokime*, which means "proven character." It is a term used to describe the process that metals endure to prove what they are really made of.[3]

On the other side of endurance, both you and others will have a clearer sense of "what you're made of." There will be a clarity of where your faith truly resides. As time passes in our lives, we begin to put our faith and wrap our identity around things—our job, our friendships, our hobbies. Suffering, enduring, and testing removes and sifts out and takes things away to reveal the true nature of your heart.

**Character development takes time**. Our character is not stagnant but dynamic. While many of us would like to assume we simply always go "up and up," this process takes time. With every fire—whether sin, shame, suffering or a combination— more debris falls away and is removed. There might be some things that get stuck. We might have repeated fires. If anything, we all have a little drama and flare to us.

But slowly, over time, this process demonstrates our potential. Fires don't hinder it; they show it. And with each fire we are put through, we acquire more confidence in our proven faith and in the power of our God.

**Our character should gradually become more like Christ**. The more we reside under pressure and endure, we are exercising our muscle of faith and choosing God's providence over circumstantial pleasure. Some people might find predictability of a person to be boring, particularly in a sitcom. But in real life, when one can be put under pressure and still stand, it demonstrates an undeniably good thing.

As time goes on, and you spend more time with Christ, learning how to walk by the Spirit, you become more Christ-like, no matter the circumstances. Like with any relationship, the more time you spend with them, the more you become like them. You begin to mimic their quirks, jokes, and dispositions. If you resemble the world's characteristics, it might be time to check where you are spending your time and what you actually believe. As we abide in Christ and walk by the Spirit, our character becomes more consistent and godly.

## Hope

While hope is often associated with a person's dreams or aspirations, sustainable hope is the final link the Bible lays out in the suffering process. This hope has some very unexpected ramifications and results.

**Hope is not risky business.** When we are in the midst of suffering, having hope can often be seen as us being naive. It can be viewed as too risky out of the idea of being hurt. Perhaps not hoping seems safer because it is the one part of yourself you can control and keep dignified. But that couldn't be further from the truth.

Hebrews 6:19 says, "We have this hope as an anchor for the soul, firm and secure." It is anchored in God's Word. The hope we have is nothing like

> Our hope is unlimited and secure in the integrity of God.

making a bargain with a genie in a bottle. That hope is limited and fleeting. Our hope is unlimited and secure in the integrity of God.

**Hope is an accurate reflection of reality.** Hope is neither a distraction nor a crutch. In fact, hope cements us into the present realities that we are in. While hope is grounded in what we cannot see, it is the concrete reality of the Christian. I have heard many times that to hope embodies an escapist mentality and is denying the present. But that's not true. Our hope is anchored in the historical resurrection of Christ. Not only has our hope been secured in history, it is secured in the future redemption of our bodies, and to deny hope is to deny a Christian reality that should fuel our souls. God can heal us in the present, but healing is always secured in the future. We never live simply in the present, not being influenced by the past or future.

**Hope is an undeniable superpower.** Hope might be seen as this flimsy and frail feeling, but it is anything but that. Neuroscientists have been investigating the science of hope for a while now because they have noticed a significant difference in people who have a sense of hope, and those who don't.

They noticed that when you experience hope (which they call belief/faith mixed with optimism), there are endorphins and enkephalins released into the brain. These actually mimic morphine, and the effects not only lead to blocking pain but boosting healing.[4]

But the superpower of hope doesn't stop there. Hope stimulates our decision-making and problem-solving capabilities in our frontal lobes, as well as our immune system, by motivating us to take action. This, in turn, shuts off the limbic system and right prefrontal cortex that holds our worries. Maintaining hope helps control our moods, not permitting us to slip into depression, and improves our compassion.[5]

We are now secured in our hope due to the love of God poured into our hearts by the Holy Spirit. This love does not put us to shame but seals our place of everlasting love and connection.

## What Does This Mean for Our Stories?

Our rejoicing is based on the supernatural power and knowledge that God has placed in our hearts. We have the secure love residing in us, confirming where our eternity resides. This allows us not only to survive but to rejoice even in the midst of challenges.

**Knowing these things, we can rejoice**. When we define suffering by God's terms and not ours, suffering is a reason for rejoicing. Suffering is not a nod toward God's wrath; instead, it demonstrates his love and how we belong to the kingdom.

Our sufferings, while perhaps not pleasant feelings, don't have to diminish or deter our joy. If anything, they increase. Because as we share in sufferings, we also share in his glory. Romans 8:17 says, "Now if we are children, then we are heirs—heirs of God and co-heirs with Christ, if indeed we share in his sufferings in order that we may also share in his glory."

This joy is not falsified, or fading into the abyss; it is enduring, the realest of real and one that lasts. It indicates our citizenship in God's kingdom. When we share in his suffering, we simultaneously share in the glory not yet seen. Even death we look forward to because of our secure future. There's truly nothing to lose. But since you're alive and reading this right now, our continuing stories can truly rejoice in our sufferings. Psalm 16:11 says, "In Your presence is fullness of joy" (NASB).

Joy is never on hold with Immanuel. It is not some lofty la-la land of an idea. It is possible.

**In our sufferings, we can be a part of the healing, hope, and rejoicing with others**. As ironic as it sounds, suffering is the most fertile soil for development and training. It equips us to become agents of empathy, healing, hope, and true joy. As we share our stories of suffering and redemption, we create a shared space for healing others. This uncanny biblical narrative has both physiological and scientific evidence to support its validity within society.

The official term is called a *redemptive narrative*. Some stories within American society include stories of liberation, the American Dream, and religious atonement. The overarching theme is that something positive comes out of the negative.[6]

This thought is also shared by counseling experts in a book called *Healing Plots*, which suggests that those who carry the redemption story have these things in common:

- Awareness that the past is a preamble for both a positive present and future
- Focused on the future, and learning from the past
- A sense of inner peace and unity
- Commitment to the next generation
- Wounded healer (alcoholics anonymous)
- Draw strength from imperfection[7]

While suffering often suggests one should be in dismay, don't let the lies of the world influence you. Brokenness and beauty are not mutually exclusive in the kingdom of God. They are invitations to share the sacred story where vulnerability and victory collide in Christ. Live your story of suffering and redemption, not swaying with what the world has to say.

## Cultivating Curiosity

1. What do you believe is the primary reason people do not suffer in the way listed in this chapter?
2. Are there any myths you believe about suffering?
3. How do you believe you can build endurance?
4. What can help you cultivate hope?
5. How can you use your past as a preamble for your current and future realities?

# NOTES

# NOTES

# CHAPTER 9

# WHAT ARE SOME PRINCIPLES THAT CAN HELP ME LIVE WELL?

*A people that values its privileges above its principles
soon loses both.*

—DWIGHT D. EISENHOWER

B EING A ROYAL HAS ITS PERKS. THINK EXTRAVAGANT PARTIES, dinner with the elite of your society, power, and prestige. It might not seem that way with all the fighting of sin and shame we do, but indeed, it has its benefits.

Being a royal also bears a high level of responsibility, expectations, and rules. The British royals, for example, have many long-standing rules and regulations they abide by, some of which include when the Queen is finished eating, you're done eating. Another one—strange but reasonable—is that any heir to the throne does not travel together in case there is a tragedy and someone passes. This will ensure the continuance of the established throne. If you want to wear a tiara, that's only for married women. Males only wear shorts until age eight, and then they can wear trousers. The royal family has its fair share of both strange and reasonable social protocol.[1]

Our kingdom, in the already but not yet, looks a little different, but is much grander. While previous and current societies might suggest that we prize tiaras or gold crowns, in God's kingdom, the crown we agree to wear is like Christ's, made of thorns. We are co-heirs with Christ as we share in his sufferings and in his glory. We are not concerned about things being passed down or not having an heir. In the kingdom of God, any Christian's death does not end the bloodline. Historically speaking, a Christian martyr most often starts something rather than ends it.

That is not the only unique thing about being a royal in the kingdom of God. Just as the British royal family has certain ways of participating in life, we have protocols that set us apart and actions we can take that help us thrive. While not an exhaustive list, here are ten principles to guide you as a royal image-bearer in God's kingdom:

## 1. Never stop being a child.

Mark 10:14–16 says, "'Let the little children come to Me, and do not hinder them! For the kingdom of God belongs to such as these. Truly I tell you, anyone who does not receive the kingdom of God like a little child will never enter it.' And He took the children in His arms, placed His hands on them, and blessed them." It might seem like a strange requirement to remain as a child, but this is a necessary entryway into the kingdom. We must take on the posture of a child, which is true humility. Babies and young children are literally helpless.

They are unable to feed themselves, soothe themselves to sleep, or communicate many of their needs. They are the epitome of someone who is utterly dependent on others.

Dependence on our heavenly Father is not indicative of our maturity. Our lives should be soaked in prayer and petitions to God not just when we believe we need whatever it is we are asking for, but because we truly need God himself. No matter how much we "mature," we never outgrow needing God. But there's more to childlikeness in the kingdom of God than just a posture of dependence. We *receive* like children too. Children who have been cared for and feel secure don't question their parents' attention and affection. Psychologically speaking, this is called secure attachment. This attachment style is when a child feels safe and comfortable around their primary caregiver. These children have unsolicited faith and trust because it has never been broken. They receive things purely, and they do it with unbridled giddiness and joy. They know they are loved and adored; therefore they receive gifts with gladness and the absence of skepticism.

## 2. Talk the old off and put on the new.

Ephesians 4:22–24 says, "You were taught, with regard to your former way of life, to put off your old self, which is being corrupted by its deceitful desires; to be made new in the attitude of your minds; and to put on the new self, created to be like God in true righteousness and holiness." This principle is one of the most commonly broken. But in order to stand out as God's heirs, we must take off the old and put on the new daily. We must throw off our sin and shame-filled selves daily and put on our new nature in Christ.

While God does not require a certain wardrobe to display his affection, our inward attitude that results in action is on display. Some of the things we should toss are impurity, greed, falsehood, slander, malice, bitterness, and all other evil. Instead, we should step into the life of the Spirit and put on kindness, compassion, truth, gentleness, and love.

If we do not daily renew our minds, being in this already-not yet world, we can easily begin to look like the world and demonstrate impatience, harshness, and jealousy in this life. But by the Spirit's refreshing discipline, we can indeed step into our new nature and be righteous and holy before the world.

## 3. Stay Salty.

Matthew 5:13 says, "You are the salt of the earth, but if salt has lost its taste, how shall its saltiness be restored? It is no longer good for anything except to be thrown out and trampled under people's feet." Salt was of multipurpose use back in biblical times, much like today in some ways. While salt is commonplace, its usage is immense. The most common interpretation of this passage points to salt's flavor and preservative nature.

Salt adds and enhances the flavor of otherwise bland food, such as pasta, bread, or potatoes. Adding salt makes it taste better and brings out otherwise dull flavors. But salt's usage is not limited to enhancing the flavor of food. Salt was also the ancient world's answer to refrigeration; it preserves the food to last longer and delay decay. We, like salt, should add goodness

> We, like salt, should add goodness wherever we go.

wherever we go. We should enhance our conversations with liveliness and encouragement, and our morality should prevent decay.

But this is in no way its *only* meaning. In the agriculture of the day, salt was also used as fertilizer for soil. Depending on the conditions of the soil, it could help the earth retain water, destroy weeds, act as a protectant from crop disease, stimulate growth, assist in making the fields easier to plow, or increase the yields. Disciples are like this. We are meant to be in places where conditions are not necessarily pristine. We can and should be in places where life is difficult, and the soil needs some love and care. As disciples, we are called to enrich the soil of others' lives, kill unruly weeds, pray against and prevent disease, and encourage growth and development. If we fail to do any of these things, we can lose our flavor.

Outside of the agriculture and food realm, salt represented something destructive in nature. It was used to express judgment on evil in ancient times. There's a sense that we express our saltiness by scattering ourselves into a variety of places—like businesses, education, the art and sciences, and countless other industries to expose evil, destroy wickedness, and stop any injustice from taking root.[2]

## 4. Be a relentless truth-teller.

1 John 1:5–7 says, "This is the message we have heard from him and proclaim to you, that God is light, and in him is no darkness at all. If we say we have fellowship with him while we walk in darkness, we lie and do not practice the truth. But if we walk in the light, as he is in the light, we have fellowship with

one another, and the blood of Jesus his Son cleanses us from all sin." Being a relentless truth-teller is a two-part ordeal. The first part means to commit yourself to a life of confession of sin. We must accept the fact that we don't have it all together and confess any darkness that resides within so that we may walk in the light and radiate God's glory. This relinquishes sin of its power as we confess and bring the darkness to the light.

The second part is to commit yourself to a life of honesty and transparency. While this might sound similar to confession, it is not the same thing. We need to be exposed and known. That could even entail sins done to us, that have us in shackles of shame.

As royalty, it might seem that not only do you have the privilege, but you also have the duty to keep up your appearance before others. But we are not supposed to keep up our worldly image-maintenance, like spinning a story to conceal the truth, or spinning it in a way that you *look good* before the world. Our love is tightly sealed by Christ, and we are known. We don't have to live a life of secrecy. Perhaps people have suggested to you that you should, but they're wrong. As in Eden, we are supposed to be completely known, accepted, and loved. Choose to be real. There is freedom on the other side of being known. When you're fully known, you're never acting in fear of thinking, *Who's going to find out?* Blackmail from the devil isn't an option. Only freedom in Christ is.

## 5. Live with God's eternal kingdom in mind.

Matthew 6:19–20, 24 says, "Do not store up for yourselves treasures on earth, where moths and vermin destroy, and where thieves break in and steal. But store up for yourselves treasures in heaven, where moths and vermin do not destroy, and where thieves do not break in and steal.

No one can serve two masters. Either you will hate the one and love the other, or you will be devoted to the one and despise the other. You cannot serve both God and money." Our life is eternal, and our citizenship resides in God's kingdom. But it is easy to look at our world and our everyday work as a way to build our empire. It is natural to want to see the potential of what could be. God did, in fact, create us to work, find meaning in it, and enjoy the fruits of our labor.

However, it is so easy to get caught up in building our own reputation, then end up serving ourselves instead of God in our pursuit of money and a comfortable lifestyle. This is not to say you cannot have money and be doing God's work simultaneously, but money is often an easy and alluring distraction that doesn't result in an eternal return.

To have and to hold an eternal perspective is to step into an accurate representation of life. Our current life is but a vapor of time. When we view our life in this way, it shifts our priorities. We can live knowing there are seasons of up and down and all that is in between. We don't have to live for the treasures of this world.

Knowing earth is not our endgame, we can throw temporary things aside and be fixated on God's kingdom and living out the Great Commission in Matthew 28:19–20, "Therefore go and make disciples of all nations, baptizing them in the name of the Father and of the Son and of the Holy Spirit, and teaching them to obey everything I have commanded you. And surely I am with you always, to the very end of the age."

## 6. Abide in God's love.

John says, "As the Father has loved me, so have I loved you. Now remain in my love. If you keep my commands, you will remain in my love, just as I have kept my Father's commands and remain in his love. I have told you this so that my joy may be in you and that your joy may be complete. My command is this: Love each other as I have loved you. Greater love has no one than this: to lay down one's life for one's friends" (15:9–13). Life is all about love. God knows we are not motivated by mere written facts; we are moved by the compelling story of Christ. Ultimate and everlasting love was demonstrated by Christ's sacrifice on the cross.

Remaining in this love produces magnificent things. We love because we were first loved by God. Biblical love is not learned or lived in isolation but in relationship with God and others. Our love also does not consist of looking in the mirror and conjuring up self-affirmation statements to make us feel better. Our love is secured in Christ.

> We can love those whom the world deems unlovable.

Once we realize that, we cannot help but overflow with love and present it in our action and attitude toward others. This abiding love changes us. It means we have the ability to forgive those who don't deserve it (because we didn't deserve it in the first place either). God just gives good gifts, and we receive them. We are no longer self-centered and self-seeking; we are others-focused. This generous love cannot help but be shared with the rest of the world. We can love those whom the world deems unlovable.

## 7. Be a lifelong learner.

Proverbs 4:5–9 says, "Get wisdom! Get understanding! Do not forget or turn aside from the words of my mouth! Do not abandon her, and she will protect you. Love her, and she will watch over you. Wisdom is of utmost importance, therefore get wisdom, and with all your effort work to acquire understanding. Prize her and she will exalt you. Indeed, if you embrace her, she will honor you. She will place on your head a graceful garland; she will present to you a crown of beauty." Proverbs is filled with ways in which one should pursue a life filled with wisdom. While wisdom is personified as a woman in Proverbs poetry, wisdom is also the person of Jesus Christ. Christ is "the wisdom of God." Pursuing the way of proverbial wisdom and the person of Christ is a lifelong endeavor; it is a never-ending reservoir of love, learning, and deeper understanding.

Embracing learning as a lifestyle does so much for you. But just to name a few: it keeps you humble, helps boredom, assists maintaining open-mindedness, and blocks you from being a know-it-all. Jesus wasn't happy with the Pharisees' arrogant and self-righteous attitude. He appreciates those who come with a humble spirit and are teachable.

As we get older or prolonged in a career, at some point we can become too proud and embarrassed to learn. But that was never meant to be the case. Learning doesn't stop once it is nixed from whatever school system you reside in. As we grow old, if we embrace lifelong learning and the pursuit of wisdom, we have the potential for a life filled with awe, wonder, and "a crown of beauty."

## 8. Know there is a time for everything.

Ecclesiastes 3:1–8 says, "There is a time for everything, and a season for every activity under the heavens: a time to be born and a time to die, a time to plant and a time to uproot, a time to kill and a time to heal, a time to tear down and a time to build, a time to weep and a time to laugh, a time to mourn and a time to dance, a time to scatter stones and a time to gather them, a time to embrace and a time to refrain from embracing, a time to search and a time to give up, a time to keep and a time to throw away, a time to tear and a time to mend, a time to be silent and a time to speak, a time to love and a time to hate, a time for war and a time for peace." If you embrace that there is a time for everything, your view on life changes.

I think one reason we are unhealthy is we demonize certain emotions and idolize others. If we truly believe that there is a time for everything, we will be able to hold the proper perspective in this world. We can have fortitude in challenging times. We can have the capacity and capability for genuine compassion. We can be human. And appreciate all the seasons that God's given us, knowing that nothing is out of place. If we embrace this overarching perspective that God has got us in this grand story of life, even if while we cannot see all of it, then we can stand firmly in faith and the sovereignty of God.

## 9. Practice Remembering.

Deuteronomy 6:12 says, "Be careful not to forget the LORD who brought you out of Egypt, that place of slavery." Being royal often comes with customary traditions. Whether that be to celebrate victories or remind ourselves of good people and good times, there are reasons for remembering. But remembering in the kingdom of God does other things for the soul that nothing else can quite do.

Remembering keeps us from forgetting. The Israelites soon forgot after God miraculously split the Red Sea how terrible it was in Egypt. They began to complain and actually *wanted* to go back to Egypt and be in captivity. They wanted to forgo the freedom the Lord provided and go back to slavery because it was a different kind of challenge in the desert.

Exodus 16:2–3 says, "In the desert the whole community grumbled against Moses and Aaron. The Israelites said to them, 'If only we had died by the Lord's hand in Egypt!'" When we become forgetful, we can easily complain about our life just like them. We can easily be deceived into believing our God is withholding good, or we are better off without God, even though he's already done so much.

Remembering can also stir our affections and produce thankfulness and gratitude for all that God has done. Studies show that gratitude lowers stress, and instills positive emotions because it is shifting our outlook in life.[3] It reminds us of God's faithfulness and shows where we once were and where we are now. It shows us that God has acted, is acting, and will continue to act in history. Perhaps this is one of the many reasons why Christ asked his disciples to take the Lord's supper in remembrance.

## 10. Celebrate!

Psalm 118:24 says, "This is the day that the Lord has made; let us rejoice and be glad in it!" (NKJV). The world presents many reasons to be downtrodden in life. Look at the news for about five minutes, and you can easily become convinced that we should not have a celebratory attitude. And heck, even our master narrative suggests evil, suffering, and sin are a whole lot to bear in this life. But our citizenship is eternal and heavenly. They're having a party. We can tap into that. Our salvation has an impact on our present, even when we don't feel it.

God created good emotions: joy, bliss, fun. He's behind all the creative minds whom you celebrate with and have fun. It is important to pause and to celebrate. Some people believe following Jesus is a life of drudgery because it takes the pleasure out of life. But Jesus is the Way, the Truth, and the Life. Christians have access to the only source of real life, and it is filled with abundance and joy. It is easy as a Christian to sometimes take ourselves too seriously in the path of maturation. But maturity doesn't mean forgoing celebration. We have the most to celebrate in this life. Perhaps not by the world's standards, but indeed we do!

These principles will guide you into a well-lived life. That doesn't mean it is trouble-free or absent of problems, but it will be more purposeful and kingdom-glorifying.

## Cultivating Curiosity

1. Which of these royal principles speaks most to you and your revealed identity in God's kingdom story? What "plotlines" does this suggest you will live out in life?
2. Which principle is most difficult for you to embrace?
3. Are there any principles you grew up with that you still abide by?
4. Would you like to add a principle to the list to help you embody a well-lived life?

# NOTES

# NOTES

# CHAPTER 10

## WWJDIHWM?

*The most common form of despair is not being who you are.*

—SØREN KIERKEGAARD

THIS IS ONE OF MY FAVORITE QUESTIONS. IT IS A TWIST ON THE classic WWJD.

Look, I'm all about the classic. I really am. Because we do need to know what Jesus would do in any given circumstance. If we choose to have our master narrative centered on Jesus as Hero, it changes everything. Jesus split our reality into an already-not yet timeline. He arrived as a baby refugee, lived a sinless life, died on the cross as the ultimate sacrifice, then conquered the grave to usher us into a new life.

Christ's life forms the foundation of our lives as God's royal representatives on earth until he comes again in history.

So there's a lot of good in the WWJD question. It is fundamental. But this twist—What Would Jesus Do *If He Were Me*—permits the question to allow for more nuances and is also truer in practicality.

We're not saying, if Jesus were *exactly* me. Then, of course, he would do whatever I would do. So there has to be something more to this question.

**If he were me**—with the same baggage, insecurities, experiences, perspectives, and heart that I currently have—**but brought to the table** an eternal perspective, empowerment, redemption, hope, purpose, then **what would the outcome be?**

If you really want to know what Jesus would do if he were you, then you have to bring your heart—your values, thoughts, emotions, perspective on past experiences, gifts and talents—in line with what he says and thinks, as revealed by Scripture. That will illuminate the path and show you what Jesus would do if he were you.

Here's how we can begin to do that:

## Identify Values

Matthew 6:21 explains, "For where your treasure is, there your heart will be also." God designed us to attach to things—treasure things, really. We were created out of divine love and creativity, and designed to reflect that. This love is insurmountable, uncontainable and must be shared.

Your values reflect *what you really care about.* Your time, energy, and focus are spent on the things you value. They represent what you believe is worthy of your worship, your time, your energy, and your life.

While God asks us to live a life of love and service as his royal image-bearers, there is no scriptural indication that we must carry an equal burden for the world.

There are things in life that you care about more and things you don't. You're not God. You're limited with your time this side of eternity, which is why it is so important to figure out what you care most about.

Take a look at this chart. We're going to revisit it at the end of this chapter with an exercise, but for now look at this list of popular values people often say are important to them:

## VALUES CHART

| | | | |
|---|---|---|---|
| Acceptance | Adventure | Authenticity | Beauty |
| Charity | Competition | Connection | Courage |
| Creativity | Efficiency | Encouragement | Enjoyment |
| Fairness | Faith | Family | Friendship |
| Gratitude | Growth | Happiness | Harmony |
| Honesty | Honor | Humility | Improvement |
| Independence | Innovation | Integrity | Justice |
| Kindness | Leadership | Learning | Love |
| Loyalty | Passion | Peace | Power |
| Resilience | Resilience | Respect | Security |
| Simplicity | Stewardship | Success | Trust |
| Wealth | Wholeness | | |

These are good things, many of which we value as individuals and as a society.

But are these really your values?

If you're really brave and are willing to take a revealing look at what you *really* "treasure in your heart," look at your calendar and your bank statement. Where you spend your time and money speaks volumes. Proverbs 27:19 says, "As water reflects the face, so one's life reflects the heart." Your life will reflect what you value no matter how intentional or unintentional you think about it.

When you do this simple exercise, it's very possible you'll discover that your daily choices are not reflected in what you say you value. This shouldn't come as a surprise since our love has been misdirected since Eden. Therefore, I would like to suggest a godly filter with which you can evaluate the things you say you value:

- What does God's Word say about that value?
- Are you living that value every day?
- Will what you value outlive you?
- Would you be willing to sacrifice time or money for what you value?

This filter will help you live every day with intentionality, purpose, and generosity. If you use it, I promise you cannot go wrong.

We were designed to care about infusing the world with beauty, love, creativity, redemption, justice, mercy, and grace toward others. But we don't all need to look the same or do the same things. We are called to *go* and spread Jesus' love everywhere, and that starts where we live every day: where we go to school, where we work, where we hang out and play. Your values can be reflected wherever you go because they are the guiding principles and beliefs of your life.

Once you have identified your guiding values, they will help illuminate how you uniquely embody and reflect the image of God. They will help you be missionally focused in your life and help assist you on where you should focus your time, energy, and life.

## Be Aware of Thoughts and Feelings

We must pay attention to what we pay attention to. On a neurobiological level, attention plays a big role in harnessing our brain's neuroplasticity (its ability to adapt, change, and form patterns). The things we give attention to, we ultimately become as people.[1] As Paul tells us, "Those who live according to the flesh have their minds set on what the flesh desires; but those who live in accordance with the Spirit have their minds set on what the Spirit desires. The mind governed by the flesh is death, but the mind governed by the Spirit is life and peace" (Romans 8:5–6).

> Pay attention to what you pay attention to, and you will know who you are becoming.

In other words, our thoughts become our master in life. Pay attention to what you pay attention to, and you will know who you are becoming.

As far as our emotions go, in chapter 2 we discussed that virtually every thought is accompanied by emotional underpinnings. I am a firm believer that God did not create robots. He invented emotions which make life both awesome and crazy at times.

At the bare minimum, we must look at our emotions as informants. When I lived in Australia, they called what you use to signal where you are going an "indicator" because it indicates which way you're turning. This is how emotions are: they indicate things to you.

I believe that when God created you—when God shaped and formed you—God gave you more emotional gravity toward certain things than others. I believe our emotional pulls can be (and are) a guide that indicates where our interests do and don't reside.

Our emotions are not an enemy to be defeated, but they are there to be understood. If we follow the mantra of "follow facts, not feelings" in the "name of God," it is very possible we just gave up a God-given indicator of what we should (or shouldn't) be doing for his glory.

I have heard so many stories of people who pursue money believing that wealth will result in greater emotional satisfaction. Scripture is clear, it doesn't work that way. So why don't you pursue what God gave you in your interests and desires? God doesn't want you to go through life without passion and purpose. Here are some questions to think about:

- What are you curious about?
- What is boring to you?
- What are you naturally drawn to?
- What brings you joy?

Chances are, when you were a child, you experienced some wonderful emotions of joy and curiosity. Consider these inklings of how you were designed and equipped by God to make the world a brighter, more lovable, beautiful, restorative place. Revisit those emotions. When you discover what God designed you to be and do, there will be affections attached to it. You'll experience positive emotions with your purpose.

Sure, your passions may evolve and change over time. Of course, there will be challenges. But what you commit your life should involve your affections of love, curiosity, and joy. Think about what you currently like or are interested in, and let God's hope and joy overflow in your heart for the possibilities of God's good and perfect plan.

## Examine Life Experiences

Your past is the preamble to your future. It is not an imprisonment or a reminder of what you did wrong. The past is a classroom we return to in order to learn, take another look, and possibly see God's perspective in it all. The experiences we go through and the stories we tell about them really do tell a lot about us.

When learning what to do, it is beneficial to examine our experiences because our experiences (consciously or unconsciously) arguably shape us the most. The past is there to be absorbed and filtered through. In going back to the classroom of the past, it is important to look at these areas to show how God has permitted the possibility of you being molded into *you*:

**Family:** What have you learned from your upbringing in life?

**Education:** What did you enjoy learning about? What subjects piqued your interest?

**Work:** What jobs have you most enjoyed? What jobs have you had the most success?

**Pain:** What have you learned through the difficulties, trials, and sufferings of your life?

Your past is a great source of information for both your present and future. In all of these experiences, you have learned both good and bad. One of these categories might have had a greater impact on you than others, but all have influenced who you are and who you are becoming.

One particular note on the last section: your greatest pain is often one of your most powerful platforms because God's power is made perfect in our weakness. So even when we are the weakest, that is a strength—and a possible indication of what to do in life. As we learned earlier, God is close to the broken-hearted. And he is keen about those being restored. He might very well ask you to use your pain to embody empathy and heal others you meet in life.

## Assess Your Gifts and Talents

1 Corinthians 12:5–7 says, "There are different kinds of gifts, but the same Spirit distributes them. There are different kinds of service, but the same Lord. There are different kinds of working, but in all of them and in everyone it is the same God at work. Now to each one the manifestation of the Spirit is given for the common good."

It is obvious God gives gifts. And they are distributed differently, for different types of work and service. These gifts are meant to be given back into the world. Take an honest look at your life and the major spheres you spend your time. At some point, you—or someone else—probably noticed that you were good at something. Talents are often confirmed by other people.

Unfortunately, your thoughts, emotions, and values might not be great at accessing this. It is very possible you have an interest in something that you're not great at. For example, I love music and I love to sing. My singing is reserved for car rides with people who tolerate it, my shower, and Jesus. Outside of this, you'll never see me pursue singing seriously.

You need to look at the experiences that life has given you. Dare to ask others who have spent time with you in key parts of your life what they believe you're good at. Ask them for honest feedback, and tell them you're not looking for flattery. This will give you a direction to pursue.

Outside of asking others, experiment with your life. Give things a try. Serve. There are many tests regarding personality, strengths, and even your spiritual gifts. But none of those are a substitute for experiencing things firsthand in service and in work. Those are standardized, and your hands-on experience is personalized. Some good things to think about is this:

- Where have I been successful in life?
- Where have I struggled or failed?
- Where have I seen fruit produced?
- What do people compliment me about?

The church is there to equip the saints, which means providing opportunities to serve and find the things you're gifted in. Once the church tells you you're gifted in certain areas, you will begin to develop and mature.

As you develop and mature, you will likely have several gifts that need fine-tuning. God has called us to pursue excellence in all we do, wherever we serve. Paul says this to the church in Corinth, "But since you excel in everything—in faith, in speech, in knowledge, in complete earnestness and in the love we have kindled in you—see that you also excel in this grace of giving" (2 Corinthians 8:7).

Excellence is our mark. Our flesh is what settles for mediocrity. With each new day, there's another opportunity to wholeheartedly serve and excel

> Excellence is our mark. Our flesh is what settles for mediocrity.

for God's glory. The passage above is most often referenced in relation to our finances, but this also applies to our life as well. Our talents, abilities, and gifts are supposed to be a gift to the world and the larger story at work. We were not created to be like a vault that keeps its treasures stored up and locked away. Instead, we were created to be like a vessel, dispensing our joy and goodness. Our gifts are meant to be marked by generosity—to be regifted and rewrapped wherever we step foot.

## Stay Curious About Life

Pursuing both life and God through the lens of curiosity provides childlike wonder and a kingdom-affirmed spirit. As you are reading this right now, you are still alive. That means you have more to learn and more to discover. Your story is still unfolding. And you have a Narrator who created you out of an outpouring of love.

If, for some reason, you're reading this now and are still not sure what you should do, then simply stay curious. God's grace is big enough for any misstep you might make. If God really wants you to do something, it will happen.

Go to God as his royal child, sit on his lap, and let him bless you—like Jesus did with the children. Ask for wisdom, for he always gives it! Jesus' brother even confirms it in James 1:5: "If any of you lacks wisdom, you should ask God, who gives generously to all without finding fault, and it will be given to you."

God is a good Father and gives generously. So continue with your curiosity-filled, question-seeking relationship, and find out what you're made for. You have a loving Narrator, Creator, and Hero alongside your adventure. There is no need to play it safe.

## So . . . What Would Jesus Do If He Were Me?

If you think about it, Jesus still hasn't come back yet. Even Jesus' story is still unfolding in this already-not yet world. And even when Jesus arrives, there's all of eternity to be continued.

It is clear that Jesus is not in a rush for things. Considering Jesus submitted himself to be human from infancy to adulthood, there is no indication we should be in a hurry either. If Jesus were you or me, I don't think he would be in a hurry to know it all or do it all. Jesus would enjoy the various parts of life—in all their stages—and appreciate them for what they are. He would go along with the process of life.

The most we know about Jesus' life takes up three years of time. He did a lot in those three years, preaching about the kingdom and ushering in a new timeline. There are several times the New Testament mentions Jesus' tiredness, and how he takes a nap or has times of solitude. Even though Jesus was mission-focused, he had a balanced pace in life. Not only is Jesus the gospel, but he also gave us the gospel. He gave his life and left love behind.

As your story continues, remember Jesus' lack of hurried-ness while remaining simultaneously mission minded. Continue through life in the process, learning as we go. Take intentional looks back at past experiences to where you are now. Consider your God-given abilities and the emotional and intellectual wiring that God gave you to then share with the world while deciding your next steps. As your story continues to unfold, leave this world by emptying yourself as Christ did, leaving a legacy of love behind.

## Cultivating Curiosity

1. Pick your top five values from the chart below. If you desire, there is extra space provided so you can create your own values. After you pick your top five, describe how you will "live your values" in everyday life (relationships, career, demeanor, attitude).

2. What are your most dominate thoughts and feelings in life right now? Do you believe they are from God, culture, friends, family, or elsewhere?

3. Examine the four areas of life experiences and write down lessons learned from them. Keep in mind that your past does not ultimately define you. We visit the past as a classroom to understand the *why* behind our demeanors, actions, and fundamental beliefs.

4. What do you believe you are most gifted and talented in? Why?

# VALUES CHART

| | | | |
|---|---|---|---|
| Acceptance | Adventure | Authenticity | Beauty |
| Charity | Competition | Connection | Courage |
| Creativity | Efficiency | Encouragement | Enjoyment |
| Fairness | Faith | Family | Friendship |
| Gratitude | Growth | Happiness | Harmony |
| Honesty | Honor | Humility | Improvement |
| Independence | Innovation | Integrity | Justice |
| Kindness | Leadership | Learning | Love |
| Loyalty | Passion | Peace | Power |
| Resilience | Resilience | Respect | Security |
| Simplicity | Stewardship | Success | Trust |
| Wealth | Wholeness | | |

# NOTES

# INTERACTIVE EXPERIENCES

W HILE I BELIEVE THE CULTIVATING CURIOSITY SECTIONS likely whetted your appetite, we all have different ways in which we learn, grow, develop and "connect the dots" in life.

In the process of writing this book, I became enthralled with the idea of narrative therapy and how it can help us view our lives in new ways. Narrative therapy empowers us to revisit circumstances and narratives, opening the door for us to consider new possibilities and perspectives. This can be life-changing.

When used in counseling, narrative therapy asks the client to look at themselves in a non-blaming (aka non-shaming) way as they restructure their views. This often takes an extended amount of time, depending upon everything you are breaking down and building up. It also needs a skilled, empathetic therapist that has both the insight to see sin and shame patterns and spot possible lies, or bad narratives.

While this book doesn't replace the experience of one-on-one counseling, the ideas in these pages are rooted in the redeeming and life-altering principles found in narrative therapy. Everything you have learned in this book so far is designed to empower you to see new possibilities and perspectives while living a shame-free, Spirit-filled life.

Now it's time to take the next step.

I want to walk you through a few interactive experiences that will help you begin to apply everything you've learned in the last ten chapters. I say "begin" to apply, because embracing healthier narratives in an ongoing discipline that will serve you well for the rest of your life.

In the following pages, you'll discover a number of guided experiences that will help you recognize and begin to rewrite your own narratives. These are tools that will help you get to know yourself, others, and the world a bit better.

# INTERACTIVE EXPERIENCE #1

# GOD'S MASTERPIECE

BELOW IS ONE OF MY FAVORITE SECTIONS OF SCRIPTURE. THIS is because of what being God's masterpiece entails. "Masterpiece" is *poiema* in Greek. "For we are God's masterpiece. He has created us anew in Christ Jesus, so we can do the good things he planned for us long ago" Ephesians 2:10 (NLT).

You might be able to tell that this is where we get the English word for *poem*. But you are not just your average acrostic poem, or even a classic kind of poem you might enjoy reading every so often. You are a living, breathing, moving soul who walks the earth.

While several poets have great imaginations, there is no imagination like God's, who creates living beings. You are God's *poiema* and God's work of art. When I hear the word "masterpiece," I often feel like it should be perfect and completely done. However, in this already-not yet world, we can (and are) both a masterpiece and an in-progress story all at the same time. Unlike an average poem, or a great one for that matter, you are like an epic that is still unfolding. Your ongoing testimony is an arsenal of truth for God's kingdom.

In the exercises below, I would like you to write out who you are as an unfolding *poiema*. Don't stress about it though. You don't have to rhyme or make it sound all fancy or proper.

Earlier in this book, I mentioned that narratives are the vehicles that connect the past, present, and future. Below is an expanded section to help you do just that. There are two ways in which you can approach the section below:

1. Freestyle and free-flow: write what immediately comes to mind
2. Label certain parts of your life in chapters, then ask:
   - "What do I call this chapter?"
   - "What would God call this chapter?"

Either approach you take will work out beautifully. You pick—it's your story!

# THE PAST

T HE PAST IS ALL YOU HAVE UP UNTIL THIS VERY MOMENT. This will likely be the most challenging part because our past is dependent upon our memory, which holds all the important events and people in our timeline. Take your time while doing this exercise.

Write about your past, including the important events, formational relationships, and the things that most deeply influenced you: the good, the bad, and all that's in between. Write about the challenges you have faced and the current strengths you now possess.

Whether or not you decide to write in chapters or freestyle, it is important to mention that Christ can "edit" *any* part of your story—via a perspective change on sin or on shame patterns, proclaiming your freedom, and providing you healing, wisdom, or any manner of abundance. Write it all down, believing God's Spirit will enlighten you as you go.

# NOTES

# THE PRESENT

W HILE THE PRESENT IS TECHNICALLY ONLY THIS EXACT moment *now*, describe your most current season in life (which can range from one week to a year). Write about your present life circumstances and your present self. How is your present self different from your past self? Are the differences good, bad, or negligible?

# NOTES

# THE FUTURE

T HINK ABOUT WHAT YOUR DESIRES ARE FOR THE FUTURE. ASK yourself these questions, then write out thoughtful responses:

- What does my ideal life look like?
- Why does it look this way?
- Who am I in the future? Think about your inward traits and outward realities. How might you be the same or different from your past and present self?

# NOTES

# INTERACTIVE EXPERIENCE #2

# WHO I AM

S OME OF MY FAVORITE PASSAGES ARE GOD'S "I AM" STATEMENTS. But Exodus 3:14 is probably both the most holy (and hilarious, based on how I read it) revelation God makes to his people for the first time post-Eden: "God said to Moses, 'I am who I am.'"

This verse translates best in English: "I am who I will be." God is self-sufficient, self-described, and all-powerful. God is defined by who he is—nothing else. God is the Creator, and we are his created masterpieces.

Back in chapter 1, I wrote a few "I am" statements that best described me at the time. In some ways, I believe writing "I am" statements can feel a little cheesy. However, they do provide clarity in who you believe you are, and for that purpose alone they are worth it.

All our vocabulary and descriptors derive from God's descriptions of us, or how other people (God's image-bearers) describe us. In this section, I invite you to do two things:

1. Reflect on the names God calls (or assigns) you. The chart below lists some, but there are several other names God calls his children.

| WHO GOD CALLS US | REFERENCE |
| --- | --- |
| **Royal priesthood** | 1 Peter 2:9 |
| **Chosen** | Ephesians 1:4 |
| **Redeemed** | Ephesians 1:7 |
| **Light** | Matthew 5:14 |
| **New** | 1 Corinthians 5:17 |
| **Righteousness of God** | 2 Corinthians 5:21 |
| **Citizen of Heaven** | Philippians 4:20 |
| **Salt** | Matthew 5:13 |
| **Adopted** | Romans 8:15 |
| **Heirs of God** | Romans 8:17 |
| **Co-heirs with Christ** | Romans 8:17 |
| **Ambassadors** | 2 Corinthians 5:20 |

2.  Reflect on what the world, your culture, your family, your social circles, and generalized society call you.

I believe the long-lasting and eternal names God calls us by not only define who we truly are in this stage of life, but they define who we will be forever. The names the world calls us by carry an obligation and a label we can't always live up to. Yet sometimes, the names our friends and family give us hold more weight than the names God gives us. We need to be alert to the names that we attribute to be most valuable and true.

In light of that, I invite you to examine: *Who do you most believe you are?*

# INTERACTIVE EXPERIENCE #3

## PURPOSE & MEANING

In CHAPTER 2, I QUOTED CODY C. DELISTRATY: "HUMANS are inclined to see narratives where there are none because it can afford meaning to our lives, a form of existential problem-solving."

This is very true. We form narratives to create meaning in our lives.

However, even in the most confident people I know, who can describe their story (past, present, future) with great detail, shout from the rooftops their sin and shame struggles while writing theologically sound "I am" statements — they still sometimes struggle with meaning and purpose.

It is important for you to reflect on whether your life must have purpose and meaning all the time. Personally, I do not believe our lives need to have meaning *all the time*. Perhaps they do, but I cannot see it or use my reasonable faculties to suggest we must live in 100 percent live-action purpose. One can make a biblical argument either way regarding that thinking, and I encourage you to do so. Ecclesiastes is the reference for meaninglessness, while God's love and unfolding story is an argument for meaningfulness.

Either way, becoming aware of your overall purpose is one primary way to operate. Living intentionally, within God's grand scheme, knowing your role in it and reflecting your talents and values—that is the best way to live. My suggestion is to look back at chapters 3 through 5 to see the different roles you have played throughout your life. Are there any that have stayed the same or changed? Then look back at chapter 9 regarding principles.

The exercise here is to generate a purpose statement that directs you in what to do (and not to do). Your purpose statement will change as you enter different life stages, so update it when you feel it's time for a new chapter to unfold, and be open to God revealing a new direction for your life.

Purpose Statement:

# CONCLUSION

Thank you, dear reader, for allowing me to take part in this journey with you! My prayer is that you have opened yourself up to new thoughts and ideas, asking yourself deep questions of the human soul. I believe the true essence of navigating life never ends. My prayer is that you have embraced the reality that we are ever-changing creations of God, who loves and encourages us along the way as new pages are penned in this expansive story.

My prayer for your life is that it may be filled with an incessant wonder that can only be cured by knowing God. I want to leave you with one last question: After reading this book and completing the interactive experiences, how do you intend to stay curious in your faith-journey?

I would love to hear about your experience with this book and your ongoing journey as you continue fostering your curiosity and choosing healthier narratives for your life. If you would like to share your thoughts with me, you can email me at k.s.williamslife@gmail.com.

# NOTES

## Introduction

1    "Journaling for Mental Health," Journaling for Mental Health, Health Encyclopedia, University of Rochester Medical Center. Accessed April 20, 2022, https://www.urmc.rochester.edu/ encyclopedia/content.aspx?ContentID=4552&ContentTypeID=1.

## Chapter 1: Who Am I? Why Am I Here?

1    New World Encyclopedia contributors, "Innate idea," *New World Encyclopedia*, , https://www.newworldencyclopedia.org/p/index. php?title=Innate_idea&oldid=1009469 (accessed April 14, 2022).

2    New World Encyclopedia contributors, "Rene Descartes," *New World Encyclopedia*, https://www.newworldencyclopedia.org/p/ index.php?title=Rene_Descartes&oldid=1022379 (accessed April 14, 2022).

3    Science Museum – Who Am I? 2010 (Exhibition)," Graphic Thought Facility, March 18, 2022, https://graphicthoughtfacility. com/science-museum-who-am-i-exhibition-2010/.

4    Staff, BibleStudyTools, biblestudytools.com. Accessed April 13, 2022. https://www.biblestudytools.com/nkjv/proverbs/23-7.html.

5    Harper Douglas, "Etymology of Existential," Online Etymology Dictionary, accessed April 13, 2022, https://www.etymonline.com/ word/existential.

6    Harper Douglas, "Etymology of crisis."

7    "Nova, Einstein's Big Idea, Einstein Quotes (Non-Flash)," PBS. Public Broadcasting Service, 2005, https://www.pbs.org/wgbh/ nova/einstein/wisd-nf.html.

8    "The Science of Curiosity," *Encyclopedia Britannica,* Accessed April 13, 2022, https://curiosity.britannica.com/science-of-curiosity.html.

9    Melissa Hughes, "3 Surprising Benefits of Curiosity and 3 Simple Ways to Cultivate It," December 13, 2019. http://info.melissahughes.rocks/neuronugget/3-surprising-benefits-of-curiosity-and-4-simple-ways-to-cultivate-it.

10   Albert Einstein Quotes. BrainyQuote.com, BrainyMedia Inc, 2022, https://www.brainyquote.com/quotes/albert_einstein_148837, accessed April 14, 2022.

11   Casey Tygrett, *Becoming Curious: A Spiritual Practice of Asking Questions* (Downers Grove, IL: IVP Books, an imprint of InterVarsity Press, 2017), 16.

## Chapter 2: What Narrative Has Captivated My Heart?

1    Rosa Escandon, "The Film Industry Made a Record-Breaking $100 Billion Last Year," *Forbes*, March 13, 2020, https://www.forbes.com/sites/rosaescandon/2020/03/12/the-film-industry-made-a-record-breaking-100-billion-last-year/.

2    McMurray, Calli. "Why the Brain Loves Stories." BrainFacts.org. Accessed April 9, 2022. https://www.brainfacts.org/neuroscience-in-society/the-arts-and-the-brain/2021/why-the-brain-loves-stories-030421.

3    Jeremy Adam Smith. "The Science of the Story," Berkeley News Blog, August 25, 2016.

4    "The Neurobiology of Why Your Learner's Brain Responds to Great Storytelling," Maestro, October 22, 2021, https://maestrolearning.com/blogs/how-your-brain-responds-to-great-storytelling/.

5    K.C., McLean & Syed, M., "Personal, master, and alternative narratives: An integrative framework for understanding identity development in context." Human Development, 2015, doi:10.1159/000445817, 58, 318–349.

6    Curt, Thompson, *The Soul of Shame: Retelling the Stories We Believe About Ourselves* (Downers Grove, IL: InterVarsity Press, 2015), 48–50.

## Chapter 3: Who Does My Culture Say I Am?

1   History.com Editors, "Revolutionary War," History.com, A&E Television Networks, October 29, 2009, https://www.history.com/topics/american-revolution/american-revolution-history.

2   History.com Editors, "Manifest Destiny," History.com, A&E Television Networks, April 5, 2010, https://www.history.com/topics/westward-expansion/manifest-destiny.

3   History.com Editors, "California Gold Rush," History.com. A&E Television Networks, April 6, 2010, https://www.history.com/topics/westward-expansion/gold-rush-of-1849.

4   History.com Editors, "Manifest Destiny."

5   History.com Editors, "Westward Expansion," History.com, A&E Television Networks, December 15, 2009, https://www.history.com/topics/westward-expansion/westward-expansion.

6   James Truslow Adams, *Epic of America*.

7   James Truslow Adams, *Epic of America*.

8   MyStorage, "Fun Facts about Self-Storage," My Storage - Richmond, Nelson, December 2, 2019, https://www.mystorage.co.nz/2019/12/02/draft-fun-facts-about-self-storage/.

9   Cary Nederman, "Individualism," New Dictionary of the History of Ideas, Encyclopedia.com, March 28, 2022, https://www.encyclopedia.com/history/dictionaries-thesauruses-pictures-and-press-releases/individualism-0.

10  Sian Leah Beilock, "Why Young Americans Are Lonely," *Scientific American*, July 27, 2020, https://www.scientificamerican.com/article/why-young-americans-are-lonely/.

## Chapter 4: What Does a Talking Snake Have to Do with It?

1   Richard S. Hess, *The Old Testament: A Historical, Theological, and Critical Introduction* (Grand Rapids, MI: Baker Academic, a division of Baker Publishing Group, 2016), 50–51.

2   Jeff A. Benner, "The Image of God: AHRC," The Image of God | AHRC, Accessed April 14, 2022, https://www.ancient-hebrew.org/god-yhwh/the-image-of-god.htm.

3    John Mark Comer, *Garden City: Work, Rest, and the Art of Being Human,* (Grand Rapids, MI: Zondervan, in association with Yates & Yates, 2017), 40.

4    Jeff A. Benner, "Hebrew Word Definition: Subdue: AHRC," Hebrew Word Definition: Subdue | AHRC, Accessed April 20, 2022. https://www.ancient-hebrew.org/definition/subdue.htm.

5    Jeff Benner, "Hebrew Word Definition: Subdue: AHRC."

6    "What the Bible Says About Dress and Keep." What the Bible says about dress and keep. Church of the Great God. Accessed April 20, 2022. https://www.bibletools.org/index.cfm//fuseaction/Topical.show/RTD/cgg/ID/2165/Dress-Keep.htm.

## Chapter 5: Why Is It Important to Have a Hero?

1    Shaun Corley, "The True Origin of Hulk Isn't What Marvel Fans Think," ScreenRant, November 29, 2020, https://screenrant.com/hulk-true-origin-bruce-banner-imaginary-friend/.

2    "Spider-Man (Peter Parker): Characters: Marvel," Marvel Entertainment, Accessed April 14, 2022, https://www.marvel.com/characters/spider-man-peter-parker.

3    "Doctor Strange (Stephen Strange): Characters: Marvel," Marvel Entertainment, Accessed April 14, 2022, https://www.marvel.com/characters/doctor-strange-stephen-strange.

4    "Captain America (Steve Rogers) in Comics Powers & Villains: Marvel," Marvel Entertainment, Accessed April 14, 2022, https://www.marvel.com/characters/captain-america-steve-rogers/in-comics.

5    Travis Clark, "All 27 Marvel Cinematic Universe Movies, Ranked by How Much Money They Made at the Global Box Office," *Business Insider*, January 25, 2022, https://www.businessinsider.com/marvel-movies-ranked-how-much-money-at-global-box-office-2021-11.

6    Dr. Eli Lizorkin-Eyzenberg, Nicholas J. Schaser, Dr. Yeshaya GruberProf. Pinchas Shir, et. all. "What Does Eve Mean in Hebrew?" *Israel Bible Weekly*, February 16, 2022, https://weekly.israelbiblecenter.com/eve-mean-hebrew/.

7    David Briones, "Already, Not Yet: How to Live in the Last Days,"
     Desiring God, April 13, 2022, https://www.desiringgod.org/
     articles/already-not-yet.

## Chapter 6: Why Am I Just Now Finding Out I'm in a War?

1    "Dunamis Meaning in the Bible - New Testament Greek Lexicon
     (NAS)." *Biblestudytools.com*, www.biblestudytools.com/lexicons/
     greek/nas/dunamis.html. Accessed 30 June 2022.

## Chapter 7: What Does New Year's Have to Do with Anything?

1    Brown Brené, *Dare to Lead: Brave Work, Tough Conversations,
     Whole Hearts* (New York: Random House Large Print, 2019), 126.
2    Curt Thompson, *The Soul of Shame: Retelling the Stories We Believe
     about Ourselves* (Downers Grove, IL: InterVarsity Press, 2015), 13.
3    Brown Brené. *Dare to Lead*.
4    Thompson, Curt. *The Soul of Shame*, 118.
5    Brown Brené. *Dare to Lead*, 140.

## Chapter 8: Wait! Suffering and Redemption Go Hand in Hand?

1    "Introduction: What Is Perseverance?" Bible.org, Accessed
     April 14, 2022, https://bible.org/seriespage/introduction-what-
     perseverance.
2    Ford, Joe. "How Much Time Do We Spend Waiting in a
     Lifetime?" AnswersToAll, January 24, 2021, https://answerstoall.
     com/popular/how-much-time-do-we-spend-waiting-in-a-lifetime/.
3    "Romans 5:4–7 Commentary," Precept Austin, Accessed April 20,
     2022, https://www.preceptaustin.org/romans.
4    Terry Small, "The Science of Hope," Accessed April 20, 2022,
     https://www.terrysmall.com/blog/brain-bulletin-47-the-science-of-
     hope.
5    Josiah Hultgren, "Why Hope May Be the Most Important Thing
     for Your Brain," MindFullyAlive, March 8, 2017, http://www.
     mindfullyalive.com/blog/2015/6/7/why-hope-may-be-the-most-
     important-thing-for-your-brain.

6     Matthew Sedacca, "How Aging Shapes Narrative Identity,"
      Nautilus | Science Connected, January 21, 2022, https://nautil.us/
      how-aging-shapes-narrative-identity-8420/.
7     Amia Lieblich, Dan P. McAdams, and Ruthellen Josselson, *Healing
      Plots: The Narrative Basis of Psychotherapy* (Washington, DC:
      American Psychological Association, 2004).

## Chapter 9: What Are Some Principles That Can Help Me Live Well?

1     Alexandra Hough, "25 Of the Most Ridiculously Strict Rules the
      Royal Family Must Follow," PureWow, August 3, 2020, https://
      www.purewow.com/news/rules-royal-family-must-follow.
2     Brett McCracken, Megan Hill, Collin Hansen, et al, "What Does
      It Really Mean to Be the Salt of the Earth?" The Gospel Coalition,
      August 6, 2021, https://www.thegospelcoalition.org/article/salt-
      earth/.
3     "Gratitude Is Good for Your Health. Here's 1 Way to Practice It
      Every Day," TODAY.com, November 24, 2021, https://www.
      today.com/health/be-thankful-science-says-gratitude-good-your-
      health-t58256.

## Chapter 10: WWJDIHWM?

1     Thompson, Curt. *The Soul of Shame: Retelling the Stories We Believe
      about Ourselves.* Downers Grove, IL: InterVarsity Press, 2015,
      p. 48.

# ABOUT THE AUTHOR

K.S. WILLIAMS holds a Master of Arts in Leadership from Denver Seminary. She is passionate about leadership, discipleship, and the upcoming generation. Two of her favorite pastimes aside from studying theology include both sports and travel. Some of her favorite games include tennis, ping pong, and pickleball (really anything with a racquet/paddle and a ball). She enjoys international travel to see friends and soak up as many cross-cultural experiences as possible. If you would like to find out more about K.S. Williams, you can follow her on Instagram @kswilliamslife or visit navigatingourlives.com.